Clearspring®

THE REAL TASTE OF
JAPAN

using the finest ingredients

Contributors

John and Jan Belleme

Ysanne Spevack

Recipes marked * by

Montse Bradford

Welcome to The Real Taste of Japan.

It has been an honour over the last thirty years to work so closely with our specialist producers in Japan. They really are an extraordinary bunch of people. Each time I visit them I am impressed by their high standards and their continued commitment to making genuine slow foods in today's hurried world. They not only uphold food traditions, they also genuinely care for the environment and their community of workers.

Another reward has been working with our contributors. So thanks to John and Jan for their extraordinary knowledge of Japanese foods, to Ysanne for her fluency in writing about them, and to Montse for her skill in creating tasty and healthy recipes.

I would also like to thank Peter Bradford for project managing this book along with our publishing friends at Cross Media, Mr Marumo, Osamu and Yukiko. And last but not least, noodles all around to my colleagues at Clearspring and the numerous distributors and retail staff who tirelessly promote our fine Japanese foods.

Christopher Dawson
Chairman, Clearspring Ltd.

Printed in UK

Contributors:
John and Jan Belleme
Ysanne Spevack
Recipes marked * by: Montse Bradford
Design and Illustration: Osamu Miyagi

Clearspring Ltd.
Unit 19A Acton Park Estate
London W3 7QE (UK)
www.clearspring.co.uk

Published by Cross Media Ltd.
66 Wells Street
London W1T 3PY (UK)
www.eat-japan.com

ISBN 1-897701-97-7

Contents

Introduction

There's something very special about Japan. A mixture of ancient traditions and the most modern of technologies. I cherish memories of a lady dressed in a traditional kimono, complete with painted white face and crimson lips, crossing a skyscraper-lined street in Tokyo whilst chatting on her tiny mobile video phone. Of pointy-hatted rural farmers ploughing the fields in the foothills of majestic Mount Fuji, as glimpsed from the window of a high-speed Shinkansen train.

There's an otherworldly approach to living, culture, spirit and, of course, food in Japan. Here in the UK, we're just beginning to explore Japanese cuisine, having been tantalised by Japanese art, philosophy and fashion for centuries. Sushi bars are springing up alongside our wonderfully rich mixture of international restaurants. Most urbanites are familiar with the bite of green wasabi paste, the mellow saltiness of miso soup, and the soft resistance of biting into stir-fried tofu. And every household has a bottle of soya sauce to hand, alongside the salt and pepper.

So why the need for this book?

Because there are Japanese ingredients and Japanese ingredients...

It's like mayo, but more so. There's mayonnaise like you get at the local hamburger joint. Then there's own-brand mayo from the supermarket. You might find the leading brand of mayo quite nice, or enjoy some of the great ready-made organic mayonnaises now available. But if you've ever tried a bonafide mayonnaise made in a home or restaurant kitchen from fresh ingredients and prepared within the last hour, then you'll appreciate the difference that I'm trying to convey.

With Japanese ingredients it's like this in terms of strength and depth of flavour, versatility, colour, aroma, and also the goodness in the product. Soya sauce is a classic example. The soya sauces readily available in the UK are mostly made with refined ingredients by a quick industrial process that produces a salty brown liquid that only faintly resembles the real deal. Clearspring, on the other hand, provide a complete range of traditionally crafted soya sauces, including the classic duo of tamari and shoyu. These liquids are full of the wholefood goodness and easily assimilated nutrients that keep you feeling good in these times of hectic activity. And they taste amazing.

Not to mention some of the great ingredients you may not have heard of before, like mochi and tekka. Mochi's meltingly soft centre and crisp crust is astonishingly delicious, and the powerful flavour of a small sprinkling of tekka provides all the kick you need to even the blandest of dishes. Lotus root adds beautiful exotica to dinners, whilst sea vegetables are bound to become a mainstay of your kitchen, whether cooking authentic Japanese dishes or just adding a bit to any of your other favourite recipes.

In fact, many of Clearspring's authentic handcrafted Japanese ingredients are so special that you can hardly find them in Japan. Take umeboshi plums, one of my personal favourite foods. Whilst living in Tokyo, I discovered these little pink balls of zingy, tasty fun and it was love at first sight. I travelled the country, popping them into my mouth as fast as I could find them. However, it was only in my last week that I finally came across traditional, artisan-produced umeboshi in a very specialist store in central Tokyo. I felt like I'd hit gold. These delicately coloured little taste-bombs are a million times more delicious than all of the other synthetically dyed numbers. The shiso herb leaves that lend them their colour are also full of nutrition, making an altogether better food.

So if traditional, hand-made Japanese ingredients are so hard to find in Japan, how come Clearspring manage to supply us lucky Brits?

Basically, it all comes down to one man's dedication and vision. Christopher Dawson is a New Zealander now living in London who is passionate about traditional Japan. Having become interested in Japanese ingredients in seventies London, he followed his heart to Japan, where he stayed for the next twenty years. During this time he worked at Mitoku Company, a trading house specialising in traditional foods. With the help Mitoku's president, Mr Kazama, Christopher travelled throughout the country, meeting traditional craftspeople and forging friendships with the individuals and families whose products Clearspring now distribute throughout Europe and the Middle East. Christopher's hands-on approach didn't come out of cynical business savvy or entrepreneurial wisdom. He simply couldn't contain his quest for genuinely wonderful and authentic foods that taste amazing and are full of goodness.

As someone who eats ecologically, Christopher selects foods that fall within these guidelines. So if you're after vegetarian and vegan wholefoods guaranteed free from genetically modified or irradiated ingredients and refined sugar, just go Clearspring. Many of the products are wheat and gluten-free too, and made with whole brown rice or whole soya beans. Most of them are certified organic, and all of them are delicious. Maybe that's why Clearspring foods regularly win taste awards, such as the Soil Association Organic Food Awards and other accolades.

It's often an outsider that has eyes to see the value in a country's heritage. Londoners blindly run around their city, missing the beauty of the architecture, the history and diversity of the culture at hand. Likewise, modern Japan has fallen for the cheapness of mass-produced foods, to the extent that many of the traditional foods imported by Clearspring are difficult to buy in Japan. Christopher has changed the destiny of some of his artisan friends in Japan. By importing their wares, these traditional crafts are now sustainable, flourishing whilst we satisfy our palates with unbelievably good delicacies. So our health is sustained along with the soil these organic products are raised in, and the communities that provide them.

So happy us, and happy them! Find Clearspring authentic Japanese ingredients at health food shops, selected supermarkets, specialist food stores like Fresh & Wild and Harvey Nichols, and online from www.goodnessdirect.co.uk.

So what are you waiting for? Dig into this book, and enjoy the very best of Japanese cuisine. It's easy when you know how...

Ysanne Spevack, London 2004

Miso

Soyabean Purée

Miso is simple to use and can enhance every course from starters to desserts. This fermented soya food is one of the world's most delicious, versatile and medicinal foods. It began appearing in UK natural food stores thirty years ago, establishing itself as an essential ingredient in wholefood cooking. In addition to its great flavour and versatility, the daily use of miso can lower cholesterol and balance the blood's pH. Unpasteurised miso is packed with beneficial probiotics and enzymes to aid digestion and food assimilation.

Traditionally, miso is made by combining koji (cultured grain or soya beans) with cooked soya beans, salt, and water, and allowing the mixture to ferment in wooden kegs at natural temperatures. Gradually, enzymes in the koji along with micro-organisms from the environment break down the beans and grain into easily digestible amino acids, fatty acids and simple sugars. By varying the type of koji used (usually rice, barley, or soya bean) and the proportions of ingredients in the recipe, traditional makers are able to create a wide range of misos, from light and sweet to dark and strong.

Misos are generally divided into two groups based on colour and taste. Sweet miso is usually light in colour (light-brown or yellow) and high in carbohydrates. It's known as 'mellow miso', 'sweet miso', and 'sweet white miso'. Because it's high in koji and low in soya beans and salt, sweet miso ferments in just two to eight weeks, depending on the exact recipe and method of aging. These misos developed and became popular around Kyoto and Japan's southern regions. The sweet, light misos or blends of light and dark misos are perfect in summer soups, dips, spreads, sauces and salad dressings.

Miso with a lower koji content, and proportionately more soya beans is darker in colour and more savoury in taste than sweet miso. It's fermented longer, at least 18 months in a colder climate. This type of miso is marketed as red miso, brown rice miso, and barley miso. Soya bean misos such as mame and hatcho are also dark and savoury. Long-aged misos were more popular in Japan's central and northern regions. Their earthy tones and hearty flavours are excellent for winter soups, stews, casseroles and sauces.

Miso was touted for centuries as a folk remedy for cancer, weak digestion, tobacco poisoning, low libido, and several types of intestinal infections. Recently, scientists in Japan, China, and the United States have discovered that miso really is effective against atomic radiation, heavy metal poisoning, cardiovascular disease, many forms of cancer, strokes, high blood pressure, chronic pain, and food allergies.

Many of soya food's healing properties have been associated with a group of biochemicals called isoflavones. These substances are particularly effective in preventing and treating cardiovascular disease and cancer. It's a little known fact that miso and other fermented soya foods, such as natto and tempeh, have over twenty times the concentration of active isoflavones as non-fermented soya foods, such as soya milk and tofu.

Miso, as a fermented food, helps your body digest and assimilate foods. Its complex proteins and fats are changed into simple, easily digestible amino and fatty acids. The same enzymes that help ferment miso can also facilitate the digestion of other ingredients in your dinner, and even destroy substances in food that cause food allergies.

Because Clearspring specialise in organic unpasteurised misos, including the popular Onozaki Barley Miso and Johsen Brown Rice Miso, the living enzymes in these misos are available to help maintain a healthy digestive system. Finally, unlike unfermented soya foods, such as soya milk, miso contains no anti-nutrients that can interfere with digestion and deplete the body of needed nutrients. Miso is a good source of some minerals and B vitamins, and its amino acids are well balanced by grains such as brown rice. Clearspring have the largest selection of handcrafted misos from Japan and Europe. Many are organic, and they are all made by the traditional process using whole ingredients and long, natural ageing in cedarwood kegs. Like the finest wines of Europe, Clearspring Misos have a deep, rich taste that only attention to detail, natural aging, and the finest ingredients can produce.

Cooking With Miso

The key to using miso in cooking is not to overpower dishes with a strong miso taste, but to integrate miso in a gentle balance with other ingredients. Darker, long-aged misos combine well with beans, gravies, baked dishes, and hearty vegetable stews and soups. Sweet white miso, with its light colour and creamy taste, makes an excellent dairy substitute for dips, dressings, sauces and spreads.

Generally, it is best to add unpasteurised miso to cooked dishes at or near the end of cooking. When adding miso to soups, for example, simply place a ladle of hot broth over the miso in a small bowl, dissolve it thoroughly, then pour the mixture back into the cooking pot. This will preserve its full, fresh flavour as well as its beneficial enzymes.

Miso Soup
Serves 4

Miso soup is one of the classics of Japanese cuisine, and is enjoyed every day in many Japanese households. There are lots and lots of variations, a few of which are given further into this book. Try this dark miso soup with added vegetables for a nutritious lunch or as a starter for dinner.

1½ litres dashi (page 48) or shiitake soaking water (page 113)

4 dried shiitake or maitake mushrooms, soaked and thinly sliced

150g chopped kale, or spring greens

1 large carrot, thinly sliced on the diagonal

3-4 tablespoons barley, hatcho or brown rice miso, to taste

Bring the liquid and mushrooms to a boil in a medium sized pan, then lower the heat to medium and simmer 5 minutes. Add the greens and carrot and simmer until they are tender. Turn off the heat. In a bowl, dilute the miso in a little bit of broth, then add it to the soup. Allow the flavours to mingle briefly before serving.

Herbed Mushroom Gravy
Makes 3/4 litre

2 tablespoons extra virgin olive oil

1 small onion, diced

1-2 cloves garlic, finely chopped

6 mushrooms, sliced

a pinch plus ¼ teaspoon sea salt

a pinch of black pepper

3 tablespoons plain flour

½ litre dashi (page 48) or vegetable stock

2 teaspoons barley or hatcho miso dissolved in 2 teaspoons water

1 tablespoon mirin

2 teaspoons fresh or ½ teaspoon dried thyme

1 tablespoon fresh chopped parsley

Heat the oil in a small saucepan, add the onion and garlic, and sauté over a medium to low heat until the onion is translucent. Add the mushrooms and pinch of salt and pepper, and sauté until the mushrooms have softened. Lower the heat, sprinkle the flour over the vegetables, and stir constantly for 2-3 minutes. Slowly add the stock while constantly stirring to stop the flour from clumping. Continue stirring until the gravy begins to simmer and thicken. Add the miso and mirin, plus the rest of the salt and the thyme if you're using dried herb. Simmer gently, uncovered, for about 15 minutes, stirring now and then. Add the parsley and fresh thyme for the last minute of cooking. Keep warm until serving. If the gravy's too thick, add a little more liquid; if it's too thin, cook it down to the desired consistency or slowly stir in 1-2 teaspoons of crushed kuzu dissolved in an equal amount of cold water. Stir until the kuzu thickens, and simmer for about 1 minute.

Shoyu

Soya Sauce

We've used Japanese shoyu in Europe since Dutch traders started importing it from Nagasaki in the seventeenth century. Barrels of shoyu arrived in Europe, and quickly found their way into the royal kitchens of Louis XIV of France. Louis XIV was a particularly paranoid monarch of that era, and as such decreed that every nobleman in the land must live with him at Versailles to stop them plotting against his reign. The palace kitchens by default became the greatest hothouse of culinary excellence in Europe, with every top chef in France competing to make the tastiest meals. This led to shoyu being foisted onto the international table at an earlier time than other Japanese ingredients, leading directly to its status today as one of Japan's biggest industries.

Needless to say, it's an amazingly versatile seasoning for stir-fries, soups, stews and salads, plus most other savoury recipes, and a mainstay of even the most rudimentary of student kitchens. But there's a world of difference between most of the stuff that passes for shoyu and the genuine sauce.

The traditional process was developed in 16th century Japan, and begins with toasting cracked whole wheat and steaming whole soya beans. Equal amounts of these are mixed together, dosed with Aspergillus culture, and incubated for three days. Now called koji, the mixture is added to brine. The thick solution of brine and koji, called moromi, is naturally aged for one to two years in large wooden kegs. Once mature, the moromi is put into cotton sacks and pressed under great force to filter out a thick dark liquid, which is a mixture of soya sauce and soya oil. The oil rises to the surface and is removed, leaving the shoyu ready for pasteurisation and bottling.

High quality traditional whole soya bean shoyu accounts for less than 1% of Japan's total soya sauce production. Over 99% is commercial soya sauce, made using hexane-defatted soya beans, fermented at high temperatures for three to six months, and containing flavourings, colourings and preservatives. An even lower grade product, called synthetic soya sauce, is often sold in supermarkets. This product is not even fermented, and is a mixture of MSG, colour additives and flavourings.

Clearspring Organic Shoyu has been made to the same recipe by eleven generations of family craftsmen. This prize-winning sauce is made with whole organic soya beans, organic cracked whole wheat, sea salt and water. Aged naturally in giant cedarwood kegs for up to 2 years, this traditional shoyu develops a deep, rich flavour and aroma that is simply a million miles better than most other soya sauces.

Clearspring have also recently introduced an authentic shoyu made in Wales. How so? A retired Japanese brewmaster was invited last year to spend nine months in the Welsh hills. He's helped establish the first UK factory making authentic shoyu in the traditional Japanese way. Although special Japanese equipment was imported, his skills were essential as much of the lengthy process involves skilled handwork. This includes the delicate art of making koji, the special culture that starts the fermentation process, and the careful wrapping of the pressing sacks where the liquid shoyu is extracted from the rich fermented moromi mash. Even more valuable, though, was the brewmaster's acute sense of smell and timing – something that had become almost intuitive after a lifetime of soya sauce brewing. By training the local food technicians into the craft of making traditional Japanese shoyu, the authentic process continues now he's returned home.

Cooking With Shoyu

In any type of cooking style, traditional shoyu enhances and deepens flavours. Only add it during the last few minutes of cooking. Brief cooking mellows the flavour and blends it with the other ingredients in the dish. If you cook it too long, shoyu's complex, delicate flavour and slightly alcoholic aroma are lost.

When using shoyu to season soups or sauces, add just a little sea salt early in the cooking to deepen and blend the flavours of the ingredients, then add shoyu to taste shortly before serving. Shoyu is high in glutamic acid, a natural form of monosodium glutamate (MSG), which makes it an excellent flavour enhancer, great for marinating, pickling, and sautéing. That said, people with MSG intolerances are almost always able to eat foods cooked with shoyu.

Scrambled Tofu

Serves 4

This quick, easy and delicious recipe is great for lazy weekend breakfasts. The sweetcorn, peppers and spring onions are optional – try different vegetables depending on what's in season.

1 tablespoon toasted sesame oil

1 onion, finely diced

1 red pepper, seeded and diced

2 ears of cooked fresh sweetcorn, or a small tin or jar of corn

2 spring onions, thinly sliced on the diagonal

400g fresh tofu

1 – 1½ tablespoons shoyu, to taste

a handful of chopped parsley

1 tablespoon toasted black sesame seeds

Heat the oil in a heavy frying pan over a medium-high heat. Add the onion and sauté for 3 minutes. Add the red pepper and sauté for a further 2 minutes. With a sharp knife, cut the kernels from the ears of corn if you're using fresh, or simply open the tin or jar if you're not. Add the corn and spring onions to the pan, and sauté for 1 minute.

With your hands, crumble the tofu into the pan, add shoyu to taste, and scramble the tofu for 5 minutes. Sprinkle the parsley and black sesame seeds, and serve hot with a crusty baguette or croissants.

Greens with Japanese Vinaigrette
Serves 4

Lightly cooked greens are full of vibrant colour and concentrated goodness. The simple dressing in this recipe complements the slightly bitter flavour of the greens. Carrots and sesame seeds add a great contrast of colour and texture.

1 large bunch of leafy greens, e.g. kale or spring greens
1 medium carrot, cut into thin julienne strips, about 2-3mm thick
1 tablespoon toasted sesame oil
1 tablespoon brown rice vinegar
1 tablespoon shoyu
1 tablespoon sesame seeds, toasted

Wash the greens and remove any tough stems or damaged bits from the leaves. Fill a large saucepan halfway with water and bring to the boil. Put as many whole leaves as will comfortably fit into your steamer or colander, and steam over the boiling water until just tender, about 7 minutes.

When the greens are tender, immediately remove them from the steamer or colander and plunge into a bowl of cold water to stop the cooking and hold the colour. Drain, gently squeeze out excess water, and thinly slice. Cook any remaining leaves in the same way.

Steam the carrots for 2-3 minutes, remove, and cool under running water. Drain and set aside. In a small bowl or cup, whisk together the oil, vinegar and shoyu with a fork. Toss the greens and carrots in a mixing bowl with the dressing. Serve sprinkled with the sesame seeds.

Tamari

Soya Sauce

Way before the development of shoyu, Japanese miso makers were using tamari, the rich, dark liquid that pooled on the surface of fermenting soya bean miso to season foods and pickle vegetables. By the thirteenth century, wet miso was being prepared on purpose, so that after fermenting the miso the liquid could be pressed and decanted. This was how Japan's small but productive tamari industry started, which today accounts for about 3% of Japan's soya sauce production.

Today's traditional wheat-free tamari is a rich, dark soya sauce made by naturally ageing whole soya beans in brine for 2 to 3 years. Its excellent cooking qualities make it a favourite of cooks around the world, but is particularly popular with people avoiding wheat.

Shoyu and tamari are both types of soya sauce. They are fermented seasonings derived from soya beans. Reduced to its simplest terms, the main difference between shoyu and tamari is the starter, or koji used. For shoyu koji, equal parts of cracked wheat and soya beans are dosed with Aspergillus culture and incubated for three days. Tamari koji is made without wheat using only soya beans and a little roasted barley flour. After the koji is made, tamari production is similar to shoyu making. The essential difference between these two sauces is that tamari is wheat-free.

Clearspring Mansan Tamari is made by the Yaemon family on the Chita Peninsula in Handa, Japan. Many modern tamari manufacturers use de-fatted soya beans, commercial sea salt and temperature-controlled fermentation in plastic or stainless steel tanks for just a few months. Mansan Tamari is made with whole organic soya beans and sea salt, traditionally fermented for up to three years in wooden casks. The time-honoured recipe uses only half as much water as typical, modern tamari soya sauces, resulting in a uniquely rich, concentrated tamari. Also, industrial tamari makers usually add ethyl alcohol to their products as a preservative. The Yaemon family brewers only add traditionally brewed Mikawa Mirin, Japan's finest sweet rice cooking seasoning, adding natural preservation and a subtle sweetness that puts Mansan Tamari in a class of its own.

Cooking With Tamari

The characteristic flavour of shoyu is a result of alcohols produced during wheat fermentation. The flavour of wheat-free tamari is due to its significantly higher amino acid content. Unlike alcohol, amino acids are not volatile, so they add flavour to foods even after cooking for a long time. Use tamari whenever you need to add seasoning early in cooking. For example, when cooking foods such as shiitake, or mild foods like fresh, dried, or deep-fried tofu, tamari is a better choice than shoyu, so you can add more flavour by simmering the mild ingredients over a longer period. Mansan Tamari's concentrated, full-bodied taste also makes it perfect for Japanese-style dipping sauces and broths.

Marinated Tofu Medley

Serves 4

Tofu picks up so much flavour when served marinated in tamari, especially in combination with mirin.

Marinade:

3 tablespoons mirin

2 tablespoons tamari

2 tablespoons dashi (page 48) or water

1 clove garlic, finely chopped

1 teaspoon of juice squeezed from grated fresh ginger root

juice of half a lemon

400g fresh tofu, cut into 2cm cubes

1 tablespoon toasted sesame oil

250g fresh mushrooms, sliced

4 cups of small broccoli florets

Mix all the marinade ingredients in a bowl. Add the tofu, and marinate for about half an hour to an hour, turning occasionally.

Heat the oil in a frying pan, add the mushrooms, and sauté over a medium heat for 3 minutes. Remove the tofu from the marinade and add it to the frying pan along with the broccoli. Toss gently, and add 2 tablespoons of the marinade. Cover and simmer for 5 minutes.

Turn off the heat and remove the lid immediately to stop the broccoli from losing its colour. Serve hot with brown rice or roasted buckwheat.

Burdock Kinpira
Serves 4

Burdock root is prized in Japan for its crunchy texture and earthy flavour, as well as its reported strong medicinal qualities. Some specialist retailers are beginning to stock it in the UK. But probably the most consistent way to find burdock roots is to simply grow them yourself. They grow very easily with next to no encouragement in most kinds of soil. Alternatively, simply use more carrots to replace the burdock.

Japanese Seven Spice (*shichimi tōgarashi*) is a mix of nori flakes, white and black sesame seeds, sansho pepper, chilli flakes, dried tangerine peel, and hemp or poppy seeds, and is a ubiquitous flavouring added to many dishes in Japan. This dish, adapted from a traditional Japanese recipe, is a simple way to enjoy burdock during its autumn and winter season.

3 medium burdock roots

1 tablespoon sesame or toasted sesame oil

2 large carrots

2 tablespoons mirin

1 tablespoon tamari

a pinch of Japanese Seven Spice or cayenne pepper

Scrub the burdock roots well, and cut into very thin, 5cm long julienne strips. Immediately submerge the strips in cold water to stop them from discolouring. Heat the oil in a heavy frying pan over a medium heat, then add the drained burdock and sauté for about 5-7 minutes. Add a couple of tablespoons of water, then cover and cook over a medium to low heat for 10-15 minutes, or until the burdock is nearly tender.

Meanwhile, scrub the carrots and cut them into julienne strips.

Add the carrots and half the mirin. Fry briefly, then cover and leave to cook. Check regularly that the vegetables are not sticking to the bottom of the pan, and if they are, stir with a wooden spoon. When the liquid is absorbed, add the tamari, the rest of the mirin, and the spices. Toss, cover, and cook briefly until tender, adding a couple of tablespoons of water if necessary. Serve hot as a side dish.

Mirin

Sweet Rice Seasoning

Mirin is a thick, sweet liquid related to sake (rice wine). If sake is Japan's version of wine, mirin is the brandy. Like sake, traditional mirin production begins by fermenting rice koji (cultured rice), cooked white rice and water for a month. However, unlike the sake making process, the white, slightly alcoholic mash is then distilled. The clear distillate (*shochu*) is then mixed with cooked sweet rice and more rice koji. After fermenting for three more months, the shochu is pressed. The resulting clear liquid is poured into ceramic containers and stored. The golden liquid that comes out of the containers six to twelve months later is mirin.

If you haven't discovered authentic mirin, you're in for a treat. An exquisite, versatile seasoning, mirin has the unique ability to coax and accentuate the flavours of light-tasting foods like tofu. That's why it's thought of as one of the three essential tastes of Japanese cuisine, alongside soya sauce and dashi (kombu stock).

Clearspring's authentic Mikawa Mirin is made by the Sumiya family. Based in the small coastal town of Hekinan, Central Japan, the Sumiyas are one of the few remaining breweries that still use the traditional process to make mirin. Most other mirins are a high-tech, synthetic blend of glucose, corn syrup, ethyl alcohol, amino acids, and salt. They are nothing like the gently sweet and silky authentic product made by the Sumiya family. Mikawa Mirin became the only mirin ever to receive Japan's coveted Diamond Award for excellence in 1975.

Cooking With Mirin

Mirin's mild sweetness balances many dishes and tones down others, such as seafoods. It adds texture and an appetising lustre to glazed foods. With a little experience, you can use mirin in a variety of ways to enhance both oriental and western cooking. Mirin enhances the flavours of sweet as well as savoury sauces, vinaigrettes, noodle broths, simmered vegetable and fish dishes, sautées and stir-fries, fried noodles, sushi rice, marinades, and dips for tempura and sushi.

Teriyaki Tofu
Serves 5

This richly flavoured and attractive tofu dish is quick and simple to prepare. It is perfect when you have unexpected guests.

400g fresh tofu

Marinade:
2 tablespoons mirin
1 tablespoon sake or dry white wine
2½ tablespoons shoyu

1 tablespoon toasted sesame oil
1 teaspoon grated fresh ginger
2 spring onions, finely chopped

Cut the tofu into five equal slices, and put it in a shallow dish. Mix the mirin, sake or wine, and shoyu, then pour this marinade over the tofu. Turn the tofu to coat all sides and leave to marinate for 15-20 minutes, turning it now and then.

Heat the oil in a large frying pan over a medium to low heat. Remove the tofu and fry on one side until lightly browned – be careful not to burn it. Turn and cook for 2-3 more minutes. Add the remaining marinade and cook for another 1-2 minutes.

Place a slice of tofu on each plate, spreading a little of the liquid left in the pan over each slice. Squeeze a few drops of juice out of the grated ginger onto each serving, and sprinkle some of the chopped spring onion over the top. Serve hot with sea vegetable salad or mochi.

Green Beans Amandine
Serves 4

Try this recipe with other vegetables such as sliced parsnips or thinly sliced cabbage instead of green beans.

2 teapoons sunflower or safflower oil

30g flaked almonds

750g green beans, topped and tailed, then thinly sliced

a pinch of sea salt

3 tablespoons sweet white miso

3 tablespoons mirin

Heat the oil in a medium-sized frying pan over a medium heat. Add the almonds and sauté for 2-3 minutes. Add the green beans and salt, and sauté for 1-2 minutes more. Add enough water to just cover the bottom of the pan. Cover and steam until the beans are tender but still have a crunch.

Mix the miso and mirin and pour over the beans. Toss and cook for one more minute, adding a little water if needed.

Baked Pumpkin with Onion Gravy*

Serves 3

You can use any variety of pumpkin or winter squash to prepare this tasty dish.

½ medium squash or pumpkin cut into thick slices

olive oil

sea salt

7-8 onions, finely cut into half moons

3 or 4 bay leaves

2-3 tablespoons mirin

1 tablespoon white miso

1 tablespoon arrowroot powder

a few sprigs of fresh parsley to garnish

Preheat the oven to 190°C/Gas Mark 5. Meanwhile prepare the onion gravy by heating a large saucepan, add some olive oil, the cut onions, a pinch of sea salt and the bay leaves. Sauté uncovered for 10 minutes on a medium flame. Cover the pan, lower the heat and slowly simmer for at least 45 minutes. The longer it cooks the sweeter it will be. At the end, add a small amount of white miso and the mirin to taste. Dilute some arrowroot with a very small amount of cold water, mix well and add to the onions. Stir for a few minutes until translucent and thicker in consistency.

Whilst the gravy is simmering, place the pumpkin slices on an oven tray. Add a few drops of olive oil and a pinch of sea salt on each slice. Cover with foil and bake in the pre-heated oven for 45 minutes or until the slices are soft. Remove and serve with the onion sauce and garnish.

*recipe by Montse Bradford

Toasted Sesame Oil

Asian cooking is full of the nutty flavour and aroma of toasted sesame seed oil. Like other oils, toasted sesame oil prevents burning and seals in nutrients when sautéing, baking, or pan-frying, but its strong fragrance and rich taste make this oil most widely used as a flavouring.

Clearspring Toasted Sesame Oil is made from whole sesame seeds that are first carefully toasted, then pressed to extract their strongly flavoured oil. No chemicals are used in processing and no artificial preservatives are added because the oil contains vitamin E, lecithin, and sesamol, which are natural preservatives. Like other unrefined oils, toasted sesame oil should be stored in a cool, dark place to retain its quality.

Cooking with Toasted Sesame Oil

Use small amounts of toasted sesame oil in marinades, vinaigrettes, sauces, and dressings, to enhance the flavour of fried noodles, and in sautéed or stir-fried dishes. Add about ten percent to give background flavour to oil for tempura or deep-frying. Toasted sesame oil may overpower some mild flavoured vegetables if used alone for sautéing, but it is delicious used in combination with another oil, such as light sesame, sunflower or safflower.

Ginger Fried Rice
Serves 2

Delicious and satisfying, quick and easy, this dish is a good way to use leftover cooked rice. It goes well with bean soup and a side dish of steamed greens.

1 tablespoon toasted sesame oil

4 shiitake or maitake mushrooms

1 small carrot, cut into julienne strips

1 tablespoon mirin

4 spring onions, sliced into 3cm lengths

1 teaspoon shoyu

3cm fresh ginger, peeled and finely chopped

350g cooked brown rice

Heat the oil in a frying pan over a medium heat then add the mushrooms and carrots. Add the mirin and sauté briefly. Add the spring onions and sauté for 5 minutes – the carrots should still be a little crunchy, but not raw tasting.

Lower the heat, and stir in the shoyu and ginger. Add the rice, breaking up any clumps with the side of a wooden spoon. Mix thoroughly, cover, and cook for 1-2 more minutes. Serve on its own or with braised tofu.

Mushroom Salad with Croutons & Fresh Herbs*
serves 2-3

The sautéed mushrooms and croutons add a richness to this simple salad. The dressing is a variation on a classic Japanese vinaigrette.

1 tablespoon olive oil,

1 garlic clove, crushed

125g mushrooms, washed and quartered,

shoyu or tamari to taste

1 tablespoon dried oregano

2 carrots, coarsely grated with a few drops of lemon juice

added to prevent from browning

½ lettuce or endive, shredded

½ cup wholewheat croutons

Dressing:

1 teaspoon toasted sesame oil

2 tablespoons fresh dill chopped

½ teaspoon shoyu or tamari

a few drops of brown rice vinegar to taste

2 tablespoons mirin or apple juice concentrate (optional)

Heat a small frying pan, add the oil, garlic and mushrooms and lightly sauté for 3-4 minutes, adding the dried oregano and a few drops of shoyu or tamari to taste.

Prepare the dressing by mixing the ingredients together. Gently mix the carrots, lettuce, sautéed mushrooms and croutons in a serving bowl and serve with the dressing on the side.

Brown Rice Vinegar

One of the world's most nutritious and delicious vinegars is made from 100% brown rice wine (*sake*) that is fermented in earthenware crocks buried in the ground. This unique thousand-year-old method survives only on Japan's southern island of Kyushu. Because it is made from whole brown rice, brown rice vinegar has a rounded, mellow taste and a high concentration of essential amino acids.

Refreshing and delicious, naturally brewed brown rice vinegar is a wonderful seasoning. It is full-bodied and sweet, yet mild, without the harsh sharpness that other vinegars often have. Brown rice vinegar adds interest to cooking, providing contrast to flavours without the need to use lots of salt or sugar.

The amino acids in this vinegar help to counteract lactic acid that can build up in the body after exercise. Despite being acidic, natural vinegar has an alkalinising effect on the blood, which helps maintain health. Excess lactic acid in the blood causes fatigue, irritability, and stiff, sore muscles plus contributes to arteriosclerosis. Naturally-brewed vinegar helps neutralise lactic acid, cleaning the blood and helping to restore balance.

Clearspring's authentic organic Kyushu Brown Rice Vinegar is made by the Maruboshi Vinegar Company, which is located in a remote area of Kyushu. With pure water, a mild climate, and premium quality rice, this company has the best ingredients for making brown rice vinegar.

Cooking with Brown Rice Vinegar

Generally, we tend to add more vinegar to food in summer. According to Kuroiwa Togo, author of Rice Vinegar: An Oriental Home Remedy, this is because more lactic acid naturally occurs in the body when it's warm. You can enjoy brown rice vinegar in all the ways you use other vinegars. Brown rice vinegar brings almost any food to life.

Besides being a main ingredient in salad dressings, pickling mixtures, and marinades, rice vinegar also perks up sauces, dips, spreads and main meals. To make beans more digestible, add a little vinegar to the cooking liquid once the beans are tender. Brown rice vinegar also adds zest to grain, vegetable and fish dishes. It can help balance salt and fats (hence the liberal use on fish and chips), and may reduce cravings for strong sweets.

Traditionally-brewed rice vinegar often contains rice sediment that can make it look muddy when shaken. This sediment is a sign of high quality.

Creamy Dill Dip
Makes about 250ml

200g fresh tofu
3 level tablespoons white miso
2 tablespoons brown rice vinegar
2 tablespoons safflower, sesame or sunflower oil
1-2 cloves garlic, sliced
1 tablespoon brown rice malt syrup
several sprigs of fresh dill

Crumble the tofu into a blender with all the other ingredients, and blend until smooth. If the mixture is too thick, add a little water or plain soya or rice drink. Refrigerate the dip for 2 hours or more to allow the flavours to mingle. It's best to adjust the seasonings after the dip has rested. Serve with raw vegetables, tortilla chips, breadsticks or as a spread.

Variation: Try using 2 tablespoons of dried onion or 3 tablespoons fresh chopped onion instead of the dill. Stir in the onion after blending all the other ingredients for a crunchier texture.

Mellow Miso Salad Dressing

Makes about 200ml

Light, sweet misos combine well with brown rice vinegar to make wonderful creamy salad dressings.

80ml sunflower or safflower oil

3 level tablespoons sweet white miso

20ml brown rice vinegar

60ml cold water

1 tablespoon brown rice malt syrup or mirin

1 rounded tablespoon chopped onion

½ teaspoon mustard powder or 2 tablespoons chopped fresh dill

Combine all the ingredients in a blender and puree until smooth. Pour the dressing into a jar, and if possible chill before serving. Shake well before pouring it over green leafy salads, sliced tomatoes, cold boiled potatoes or sea vegetable salad.

Sea Vegetable Salad*
Serves 2-3

This mixture of land and sea vegetables makes a colourful and nutritious salad.

⅓ cup dulse

⅓ cup wakame

½ cucumber finely sliced

1 cup cherry tomatoes, cut in half

⅓ lettuce shredded

½ cup of cooked sweetcorn kernels

Dressing:

3 tablespoons water

2 tablespoons brown rice vinegar

2 tablespoons shoyu or tamari

1 tablespoon olive oil

1 tablespoon orange zest

1 teaspoon prepared mustard

Rinse the wakame and dulse sea vegetables under cold water then soak the dulse for 1 minute and wakame for 3 minutes, drain and cut into pieces. Prepare the dressing by blending together all the ingredients, adding some to the cut sea vegetables. Wash and cut the remaining salad ingredients, then mix with the sea vegetables and gently toss together with enough of the dressing to suit your taste.

Ume Plum Seasoning

Ume-Su

Ume Plum Seasoning is called *ume-su* in Japan. Although this translates as 'plum vinegar', it's actually the pickling brine drawn from kegs of umeboshi. This pleasantly tart and salty purply-pink liquid is a versatile and delicious seasoning, with all the fruitiness and health benefits of umeboshi plums (page 83).

Cooking with Ume Plum Seasoning

Use Clearspring Ume Plum Seasoning to liven up salad dressings, cooked vegetables, homemade quick pickles, and tofu spreads. Add a teaspoon to a bowl of sliced radishes or cucumbers then toss and leave for about fifteen minutes before serving as a zesty side dish. Ume plum seasoning is especially good with leafy greens, cauliflower, broccoli and green beans. Steam, boil or sauté the vegetables until tender but still firm. Drain if necessary, place in a serving bowl and toss with ume plum seasoning to taste. When substituting ume plum seasoning for vinegar, reduce or eliminate the salt in the recipe. Try adding a few drops to chilled sparkling water for a refreshing summer drink.

Guacamole

This quick and easy recipe makes a delicious spread for toast, crackers, or flatbread, or as a dip for sticks of celery or cucumber. Make it just before serving to ensure it keeps its green colour, using soft, ripe avocadoes. The skin should peel easily and the flesh easy to mash.

1 large or 2 small ripe avocadoes, peeled and pitted
¼ of a small onion, grated
1 tablespoon ume plum seasoning
the juice of ¼ lemon
a sprig of parsley, finely chopped

Mash the avocadoes with a fork. Add all of the other ingredients, and mix well with the fork.

Serve immediately with hot pitta bread and olives.

Tagliatelli with Home-made Pesto*

Serves 2

Ume plum seasoning and white miso give this pesto a tangy and creamy quality as an alternative to cheese.

½ pack wholewheat or white tagliatelli

a pinch of sea salt

Pesto:

½ cup fresh parsley

¼ cup fresh basil

1 tablespoon olive oil

1 garlic clove, minced

3 tablespoons ume plum seasoning

2 tablespoons white miso

½ cup of ground almonds

Cook the pasta in your usual way, then rinse quickly under cold water and drain.

Finely cut the fresh herbs and blend with the rest of the ingredients, adding just enough water if needed to give you a thick sauce consistency. Serve over the cooked pasta.

Dashi

An essential ingredient in Japanese cuisine is dashi. It's an earthy flavoured stock made from kombu soaking water. It's a great base for soups, stews, sauces, noodle broths and dips for tempura. Usually dashi is seasoned to taste with a generous serving of shoyu. Often mirin is also added, plus a little juice squeezed from a piece of grated ginger root.

To prepare a basic dashi, soak two 15cm pieces of kombu and three dried shiitake or maitake mushrooms in about 2 litres of water for at least 15 minutes. Remove the mushrooms, and thinly slice the caps. Then return them to the water, bring it to the boil and simmer gently for 10 minutes. Remove the kombu and keep it to use for cooking as a condiment or with beans.

Noodles in Broth with Onion Ring Tempura*
Serves 2

1 pack soba or udon noodles
2 onions, cut into half moons
1 carrot, cut into matchsticks
1 x 15cm strips of kombu sea vegetable
1-2 teaspoons juice squeezed from grated fresh ginger
tamari or shoyu and mirin or apple juice concentrate to taste
fresh watercress to garnish

Onion Ring Tempura:
1 medium onion, thinly sliced and separated into rings
Clearspring Sunflower Frying Oil for deep frying
tamari or shoyu
1 cup plain flour
3 tablespoons arrowroot powder
a pinch of sea salt
1 teaspoon roasted sesame seeds
some sparkling water.

Cook the noodles (see page 77), rinse and drain. Boil 1½ litres of water with the kombu strips for 20 minutes. Add the onions and simmer uncovered for 10 minutes. Add the carrots and simmer 3 minutes. Season with tamari and mirin. To make the onion ring tempura, combine the flour, arrowroot, salt and sesame seeds, add some water and mix thoroughly into a smooth batter. Place in the fridge for one hour. Heat a frying pan with enough oil for deep frying. Submerge each onion ring into the batter and deep fry for 2-3 minutes until lightly golden and very crisp. Remove each ring and drain on a paper towel. To serve, fill individual bowls with the cooked noodles and cover with the hot broth. Top with the tempura onion rings garnished with watercress.

Sea Vegetables

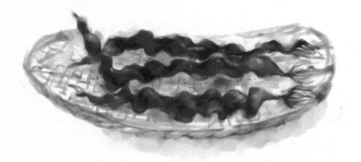

Sea vegetables contain more minerals than any other kind of food. All of the elements essential for human health – including calcium, magnesium, potassium, iodine, iron, and zinc together with important trace elements that are often lacking in land vegetables due to soil demineralisation are present in sea vegetables. Calcium, iron and iodine are particularly important to people eating dairy-free or vegetarian diets. For example, half a cup of cooked hijiki contains more calcium than a whole cup of milk and double the amount of iron than an egg. Iodine is rare to find in most foods. However, sea vegetables are rich in this essential mineral.

Harvesting plants from the sea may seem a novel idea, but many varieties of sea vegetables have been eaten since the year dot. And for good reason... Properly prepared, high-quality sea vegetables are delicious. They're also really handy, as unlike most land vegetables, they are stored dry for use whenever you need them.

If you're watching your weight, sea vegetables could be the answer for you. They're high in fibre and next-to-no-calorie, but deliver the minerals you need to keep you healthy. Over the last few decades, medical researchers have discovered that a diet rich in sea vegetables reduces the risk of some diseases and helps the body eliminate dangerous toxins. In fact, surveys show that people living in areas where sea vegetables are regularly eaten tend to live longer, healthier lives. The rule of thumb with sea vegetables is eat a little and often. Keep a pack of Clearspring Green Nori Flakes with your herbs and spices, and experiment by adding to savoury dishes.

Hijiki and Arame

Hijiki looks like thick, black, lustrous hair as it grows on the ocean floor, waving in the currents. Minerals are essential for healthy hair, and hijiki has a very high mineral content. Clearspring Hijiki is harvested along the Boshu peninsula on the east coast of Japan's main island, and is Japan's premium hijiki. The mild climate of Boshu is ideal for this sea vegetable, which flourishes along the rocky coastline.

Clearspring Hijiki is harvested and prepared in the traditional way. It's harvested in the early spring, just as it reaches its peak flavour. After it's washed, the entire plant is steamed for nine hours in its own juices. Left overnight to cool, it's then thoroughly air-dried before being packaged. This simple traditional process isn't generally used anymore in Japan for most commercially available hijiki. These days, hijiki is boiled in water for long periods, resulting in a weaker flavour and less minerals in the final product.

Like hijiki, arame is a brown seaweed, but it grows in deeper waters and has a much milder taste. Clearspring Arame is gathered off the Ise peninsula, the site of one of Japan's most famous shrines. In late summer, local fishermen wade out to gather the young, tender plants at low tide, or dive into shallow waters and cut the arame from the seabed. The plants are then finely shredded and processed in a similar way to Clearspring Hijiki. Arame and hijiki are both great sources of iron and calcium.

Cooking with Hijiki and Arame

When properly cooked and presented, hijiki looks stunning. Its shimmering black colour adds superb contrast and beauty to any meal. Cold hijiki salad topped with a creamy white tofu dressing and a sprinkle of finely chopped spring onion or parsley looks fantastic on a hot summer day.

Although hijiki and arame are prepared in similar ways, there are a few important differences. Hijiki is thicker and coarser, and has a strong ocean flavour that some people find a bit overpowering. Arame's milder aroma and taste make it a better choice for anyone just beginning to use sea vegetables.

Both need to be rinsed quickly but carefully to remove any sand or shells, then soaked in water. Because of the difference in their textures, hijiki should be soaked for ten minutes, while the more delicate arame needs only five minutes.

Soaking triples the size of arame and hijiki. It's generally best to squeeze out excess water after soaking. Then add soaking water or fresh water to almost cover and simmer until it's tender and most of the liquid is absorbed. This will be about twenty minutes for hijiki and fifteen minutes for arame. Finally, season the tender sea vegetables with shoyu and mirin, and cook for a few more minutes.

Both cooked hijiki and arame are delicious when sautéed with sweet vegetables such as carrots, slow-cooked onions or pumpkin. They also combine well with tofu or tempeh. Hijiki and arame are great in salads, especially when topped with a tofu dressing.

Hijiki with Shiitake, Carrot and Dried Tofu

Serves 4-5

This recipe is for hijiki, but simply adjust the soaking and cooking time as described in the previous section if you want to try it with arame instead.

50g hijiki

2 teaspoons sesame oil

4-5 dried shiitake or maitake mushrooms, soaked for 2 hours, then sliced

4 pieces dried tofu

2 tablespoons shoyu

1 tablespoon mirin

1 carrot, sliced thinly on the diagonal

a handful of chopped fresh parsley

Wash the hijiki, then add water to almost cover it and simmer for about 35 minutes. Heat the oil in a frying pan, add the sliced mushrooms, and sauté for 2 minutes. Carefully drain the hijiki in a colander, keeping the soaking water to use as a stock another time. Add the hijiki to the pan and sauté for another 2 minutes. Add the mushroom soaking water plus some fresh water to almost cover the vegetables, then bring to a boil, lower the heat, and leave to simmer with the lid on.

Meanwhile, soak the dried tofu for 5 minutes, then squeeze out the excess water. Dice it, and add to the hijiki, mixing well. Simmer for 30 minutes. Mix in the shoyu and mirin, then put the carrots on top of the hijiki mixture, cover the pan, and cook for 10 more minutes. Mix well. If there's still any liquid, cook uncovered over a medium heat for a few minutes until it's nearly dry. Sprinkle the parsley over the top, then cover and cook for 1 more minute.

Serve with pan-fried mochi or as a filling for pitta bread.

Arame Summer Salad*
Serves 4-6

Long summer days are an ideal time to make the most of fresh sweetcorn. Try this salad for a perfect lunch, or as a side dish.

30g arame, soaked in cold water or 10 minutes and drained

1 tablespoon shoyu

3 ears of fresh sweetcorn or ½ cup frozen sweetcorn kernels

2 cups mangetout or fresh green beans

a handful of bean sprouts

2 grated carrots with lemon juice added to prevent browning

Dressing:

4 tablespoons coarse grain mustard

2 tablespoons tahini

3 tablespoons brown rice vinegar

100ml boiling water

If you're using fresh sweetcorn, steam until the kernels are tender. Remove the corn from the water, and allow it to cool, then remove the kernels from the cobs. If you're using frozen corn, boil for 2-3 minutes and rinse.

Boil the mangetout or green beans for 4-5 minutes, wash under cold water and drain. In the same water blanch the bean sprouts for 5 seconds, rinse under cold water and drain.

In a serving bowl, mix the arame, corn, mangetout or green beans, bean sprouts, and grated carrot. Blend the dressing ingredients together until smooth, in a blender. Add the dressing to the salad, mixing well. Serve with tabouleh salad or cold Japanese noodles.

Nori

Along the northeast coast of Japan, in the Sendai region, are the idyllic pine-covered islands of Matsushima. This pure, cold-water coastline is home to a seemingly endless stretch of quiet coves and sheltered shallows, the perfect place to grow nori seaweed. Japanese nori is the best-known sea vegetable in the West, dried and pressed into thin sheets used to wrap around sushi.

Although originally gathered wild, nori has been cultivated in Japan for over 300 years. Nets made of woven rope are suspended between long bamboo poles set deep into the gentle bays. During the cold winter months, nori slowly grows until it covers the entire net. The nets are placed so that they remain above the water level during low tide, giving the growing nori maximum sunlight, yet regular washing below the water level during high tide. In January and February, this fragile, green seaweed is gathered from the water by hand and brought ashore. There it's washed, first in sea water, then in fresh water. It's finally put on bamboo mats to dry slowly and carefully, a process that's just like hand making paper.

Like many foods in Japan, nori is available in various different qualities. Lesser grades of nori are a dull, purplish-black and lack Clearspring Nori's vibrant sheen. Clearspring Nori is a choice grade. Its fine, even texture and translucent, deep-green colour are the proof of its excellence.

Cooking with Nori

Except for sushi nori, which comes ready-toasted, nori needs to be lightly toasted before use. Be careful when toasting it, as nori is delicate and burns easily. Simply hold the unfolded sheet briefly over a gas flame or electric burner and watch as the colour magically changes to a brilliant bright green as it becomes crisp and fragrant.

Nori is most commonly used to wrap around rice balls, which are sort of the Japanese version of sandwiches. Nori is also used to wrap other foods, such as *maki-sushi*. Cut into short strips, nori is delicious wrapped around bite-sized clumps of warm rice dabbed with umeboshi paste. Crumbled or cut into strips, nori can be used to season soups and vegetables, or grain and noodle dishes.

Nori is also used in Japan as a party food that's a variation of *nori-maki* called *te-maki*, literally meaning 'wrapped by hand'. A quarter sheet of toasted nori is topped with a little sushi rice or noodles along with an assortment of foods such as avocado or other vegetables. Flavourings such as umeboshi or wasabi can be added, then the nori is rolled into a funnel or cone shape. *Te-maki* make stylish finger food for parties, especially when served with hot sake.

Another variety of nori is sold in flake form. Green Nori Flakes make an attractive herb-like garnish or seasoning for fried rice and noodles, other grain dishes and salads. Green Nori Flakes are the richest type of nori in iron and protein.

Crunchy Nori Bundles with Peanut Dressing*

Serves 2

Try this as a packed lunch or for picnics.

2 medium carrots, cut into long strips about ½ cm thick

½ cucumber, cut lengthwise into strips like the carrots

1 sheet nori

Dressing:

1 tablespoon peanut butter

1 teaspoon mustard

an orange, squeezed

1 teaspoon barley miso

Steam the carrots for 3-5 minutes, until they're tender, then rinse under cold water and drain. Toast the nori by carefully holding the sheet horizontally 5cm above an open flame using tongs, then gently rotating it for a few seconds until its colour changes to a vivid green. Cut the sheet using kitchen scissors into four equally sized strips.

Take two pieces of each vegetable and wrap one strip of nori around each bundle. Use a drop of water to seal the ends. Repeat the process with the other three bundles, then arrange them in a serving dish.

To make the dressing, mix all the ingredients together in a cup with a fork. Add a little water if the paste is too thick. You're aiming for a loose and creamy dressing. Serve on the side, or drip around the dish in a spiral to serve.

Stuffed Nori Cones*

Makes 8 cones

Known as *te-maki* in Japan, these cones are a quick and easy starter, and are fun for parties too.

2 sheets toasted nori

100g cooked brown rice

a handful of chopped watercress

a large carrot, grated

4 tablespoons toasted sesame seeds

juice of half a lemon

1 tablespoon coarse grain mustard

1 tablespoon ume plum seasoning

watercress sprigs for garnish

With scissors, cut each nori sheet into four quarters. Place all the remaining ingredients in a bowl and mix together well. Taking one piece of nori at a time, carefully roll it into a cone. Use a drop of water on your finger to stick the overlapping sides together. Just before serving, fill each cone with the mix, decorating the top of each one with a sprig of watercress.

Wakame

Wakame is a staple food in the traditional Japanese diet. It is a dark green sea vegetable that grows at depths of about two metres, and thrives in cold, strong ocean currents. The taste and texture of different varieties of wakame vary. Unlike most wakame on the market, which has a strong ocean flavour and relatively rough texture, Clearspring Wakame is a high grade and has a mild taste and delicate texture. It's simply delicious, with a springy texture. It's high in calcium, iron and iodine, as you'd expect from a vegetable that's been grown in mineral-rich sea water. Plus it contains A and B vitamins.

Clearspring Wakame comes from the remote San-Riku coastline of northeastern Japan, renowned for its superb seafood. The cold Pacific waters are clean and clear, providing the perfect environment for growing wakame that is particularly tender and tasty. The harvest takes place in early spring, from February until the end of March, as the plants reach maximum size, and before their leaves start to harden. The wakame is briefly washed, then hung up for several days until it is completely crisp and dry.

Cooking with Wakame

Soak dried wakame in lukewarm water for ten minutes. Remove, squeeze out the excess moisture, cut away any tough ribs, and slice. Wakame is especially good in soups and salads. It can also be added to stews and vegetable or bean dishes. As it's delicately flavoured and tender, it shouldn't be cooked for more than a few minutes.

Try toasting dried wakame in a dry frying pan or in the oven to make a condiment, but be careful not to burn it. Once toasted, the wakame is crumbled or ground into a powder in the same way as making Roasted Kombu Condiment (page 68). Toasted sesame seeds may be added and ground with the toasted wakame. This mixture is excellent sprinkled over grains, tossed with cooked rice, or added as a seasoning to soups and salads.

For a cooling and exotic salad, combine chilled wakame with sliced cucumber or orange and a vinaigrette.

Watercress with Scrambled Tofu*

Serves 2-3

1 tablespoon sunflower or safflower oil

1 block of fresh tofu, crushed with a fork

1 tablespoon sweet white miso mixed with 1 tablespoon water

30g wakame, soaked for 3 minutes, then cut into small pieces

3 bunches of watercress

fresh kernels from one ear of sweetcorn, cooked or a tin of sweetcorn, drained

the juice of 3cm freshly grated ginger root that's been squeezed

3 tablespoons sesame seeds, roasted

Heat the oil in a large frying pan over a medium heat, add the tofu and stir constantly for 2-3 minutes. Add the miso and mix well. Add the wakame, watercress and sweetcorn and sauté for 1-2 minutes. Add the ginger juice and seeds, mix in and serve with a crusty baguette.

Wakame White Miso Soup
Serves 4

The golden colour and light, sweet flavour of this nutritious soup makes it a good choice during the warmer months.

30cm piece of wakame

1½ litres dashi (page 48) or vegetable stock, or water

1 large or 2 medium carrots, thinly sliced

6 small spring onions, cut into 1cm pieces

80g sweet white miso

Soak the wakame for 10 minutes, cut away any tough ribs, and slice the fronds into 2cm pieces. While it's soaking, bring the dashi or stock to the boil, add the carrots, and simmer for 10 minutes. Add the spring onions and simmer for a few more minutes. Add the wakame to the soup, simmer for 2 minutes, then remove from the heat.

In a cup, thin the miso with a little bit of the hot soup, then add this liquid back into the pan. Stir the miso in well, then leave the soup for a couple of minutes so that the flavours can mingle.

Kombu

In the cold seas off Hokkaido, Japan's northernmost island, a brown algae known as kombu (kelp), grows in a dense underwater forest. Swaying with the rhythm of the sea, individual fronds reach up from the ocean floor sometimes to a height of over thirty feet. There are many different grades of kombu gathered from Japan's clear arctic waters, but Clearspring Kombu from Hidaka province is generally recognised as the best. Kombu is ready to harvest in late summer. Floating on the water in small boats, men and women cut the kombu free using razor-sharp knives attached to long bamboo poles. As the kombu floats to the surface, it is gathered with wooden rakes and hauled into the boats. Once back on land, it is laid out to dry slowly and naturally in the sun.

The broad flat blades and deep, even colour of Hidaka kombu are the signs that it's top quality. The white mineral powder on kombu's dried surface contains the natural glutamic salts that help make kombu a powerful flavouring agent, able to bring out the flavours of the other ingredients in your recipe. Don't wash off the powder. Simply wipe the kombu with a damp cloth before use.

Cooking with Kombu

Kombu can be used in clear soups, cooling salads, hearty stews and vegetable dishes. In most recipes, you don't need to soak kombu before use. If you do need to soak it for a salad or stir fry, just put it in luke-warm water until it softens and opens up. Make sure you keep the soaking water for use at a later time in soups or stews. Whenever you're cooking beans, add a piece of kombu. It helps soften the beans, reduces cooking time, and makes them easier to digest.

Kombu's most common use is in the preparation of dashi, Japan's multi-purpose stock for soups, stews, and sauces. Dashi is simple to make, and it is integral to Japanese cooking, since it is the first step in many traditional dishes. See page 48 for a simple and authentic dashi recipe. Try also making the easy Roasted Kombu Condiment over the page, as sprinkled on dinners throughout Japan.

Roasted Kombu Condiment

This condiment can be added as a seasoning to soups, or sprinkled over grains and vegetable dishes before serving. Simply cut some kombu strips into small pieces. Place in a wok or frying pan over a medium heat with no oil. Stir the kombu pieces constantly until they become very crisp. Pour the roasted kombu pieces into a mortar, bowl or suribachi (Japanese grinding bowl), and grind the kombu into a fine powder using a pestle or wooden spoon. Alternatively, wait for the kombu to cool, and put the pieces in a transparent plastic bag. Then crush them into a powder using a rolling pin or a handy wine bottle.

For a tasty and nutritious variation, add toasted sesame seeds to this condiment. You can use any proportion of seeds to the kombu, to suit your taste. In a small dry frying pan, toast the sesame seeds over medium heat, stirring constantly, for 1 to 2 minutes, or until they are fragrant and begin to pop. Remove from the heat immediately, as they become bitter if overcooked. Add the seeds to the mortar or suribachi along with the roasted kombu and grind them together.

Hearty Baked Vegetables
Serves 3-4

This warming dish, with its attractive autumnal colours, is great as the days become cooler.

15cm strip of kombu soaked in 250ml cold water for at least 10 minutes

1 large onion, halved and sliced into wedges

½ a head of cabbage, sliced into 1cm wedges

2 - 3 large carrots, cut into small bite-sized chunks

½ winter squash or pumpkin, cut into bite-sized chunks

1 tablespoon shoyu

Preheat the oven to 190°C / Gas Mark 5. Take the kombu out of the soaking water. Keep the soaking water, and cut the kombu into 2cm pieces. Put all of the vegetables into a casserole dish.

Add the shoyu to the kombu soaking water and pour over the vegetables. Cover and bake until tender, about 50-60 minutes. Serve hot with brown rice.

Sea Vegetable Salad

Clearspring's ready-mixed Sea Vegetable Salad is an instant winner. This special blend of sea plants includes a delicate and tender grade of green Japanese wakame, translucent agar-agar strips, and slivers of red algae. Not only does it provide lots of minerals, but when soaked and served, it's sure to be a show-stopper. The combination of translucent, leaf green and deep red strands is just beautiful, and the delicate flavours complement lots of different main courses. Keep a pack handy for unexpected salad nights.

This eye-catching salad couldn't be easier to prepare. Simply soak the dried sea vegetables in warm water for ten minutes, then drain, rinse briefly, and squeeze out excess water. Note that the volume of the salad will expand about eight to ten times as it soaks. Enjoy as a salad by itself or combine it with fresh lettuce and other vegetables for the best of land and sea. Serve Sea Vegetable Salad with the Tofu Sesame Salad Dressing shown here, try it with a Japanese vinaigrette of shoyu, sesame oil, mirin and brown rice vinegar, or simply use your favourite salad dressing.

Tofu Sesame Salad Dressing

This dressing is excellent with Sea Vegetable Salad, because its sweet and sour taste brings out the delicate flavours of the vegetables. It is also good on tossed salad and hijiki salad.

150g fresh tofu

60ml safflower or sunflower oil

1 tablespoon toasted sesame oil

3 tablespoons brown rice vinegar

60ml water

3 level tablespoons sweet white miso

1 clove garlic

1 tablespoon brown rice malt syrup

1 tablespoon brown or black sesame seeds

Blend all the ingredients except the sesame seeds, or mix well with a fork. Toast the seeds in a dry frying pan by stirring constantly over a medium heat for 2-3 minutes. Pour the dressing into a bowl, mix in the seeds, and chill slightly before serving. Try this dressing with freshly chopped parsley.

Noodles

Noodles are the Asian version of pasta... Actually, pasta is the Italian version of noodles, inspired by the Chinese noodles brought back to Europe by Marco Polo. Probably more noodles are eaten in Japan today than any other food except rice. Quick and simple to prepare, delicious and satisfying, Japanese-style eggless noodles are a staple food. They're served very differently in Japan than the pastas we know so well. During summer, noodles are refreshing served floating in a bowl of ice water with a chilled dipping sauce on the side. For warmth in winter, they are served in a piping hot broth. Whether in soups or salads, sautéed with vegetables, deep-fried, baked, or topped with sauce, noodles are delicious. In the time it takes for the water to boil and the noodles to cook, you can prepare a soup, sauce or vegetable dish and voilá! In twenty minutes there's a nutritious and delicious meal.

The Making of Authentic Japanese-style Noodles

In the rolling grasslands of remote northeast China, farmers have grown grains and beans from traditional seed varieties for four thousand years. Their fertile land has never known chemicals. Nearby, in the mountain-fringed Yanqing Lake District, award winning miller and Japanese pasta maker, Takao Ogura, found the perfect location to set up his grain mill and traditional noodle shop to make Japanese-style noodles. Using pure spring water and locally grown, freshly milled organic flours, Ogura-san uses the traditional roll-and-cut method and natural air-drying to make noodles of incomparable taste and quality. He begins by adding salted water to freshly stone-ground organic flour. The correct salt content is critical for developing the right amount of protein in the dough and to make sure the noodles stay fresh. The dough is thoroughly mixed and kneaded, then allowed to rest.

After several hours, the dough is checked for the right level of stickiness. It's then passed through a series of rollers to form thin, long sheets. The last roller has a cutter attached, which can be changed to cut the dough into different thicknesses and shapes for soba, lomein or thick traditional udon noodles. Whether flat or round, thick or thin, the long strands emerging from the cutter are chopped into six-foot sections and carried to a special drying room. From start to finish, Ogura-san's noodle-making is based on the way noodles are made at home.

After drying for at least thirty hours, the noodles are cut for packaging. The whole process takes about four times as long as the modern method, which can be completed in an eight-hour day.

Clearspring Noodles are quick cooking, and the farms, mill and noodle shop are all certified organic.

Organic Lomein

Lomein is the original spaghetti introduced to Europe on Marco Polo's return from the East. Traditional wheat pasta is still one of the world's most wholesome and versatile convenience foods. Although most commonly associated with Japanese, Chinese, Thai and other Asian recipes, lomein is great for Italian pasta dishes as well.

Organic Udon

These smooth, traditional, thick Japanese wheat noodles are quick cooking and versatile. They're ideal for Japanese noodle dishes, and can make a delicious change for Italian fettucini recipes.

Organic Brown Rice Udon

These noodles are made from a mixture of brown rice and wheat flours. Their smooth texture and satisfying flavour can be used in any recipe needing udon or lomein.

Organic Soba

Soba noodles are made from freshly milled buckwheat and wheat, giving them a rich and nutty taste. They're best suited to Japanese and Chinese dishes. Soba comes in different percentages of buckwheat to wheat, including a 100% buckwheat soba made by the Sakurai family in Japan, which is ideal for people seeking to avoid wheat. Buckwheat is popular in Eastern Europe although it actually originates in China. It is not related to wheat.

Organic Jinenjo Soba

Jinenjo is a mountain yam root known in Japanese folklore for its strengthening and rejuvenating qualities. Clearspring Jinenjo Soba is made by the Sakurai Family in Japan using a mix of ground jinenjo root, wheat flour and buckwheat flour. It has a distinctive taste and smooth texture.

Cooking Japanese Noodles

Since most Japanese noodles are made with salt, you don't need to add salt to the cooking water. You need about 2.5 litres boiling water to every 250 gram pack of noodles. Add the noodles a few at a time so the water doesn't stop boiling. Stir gently until the water is boiling rapidly again to prevent the noodles from sticking to the bottom of the pan. If too many noodles are added at once, the water won't return to the boil quickly enough, and the noodles will overcook on the outside and undercook on the inside. Also, using too little water will result in sticky, unevenly cooked noodles.

Some Japanese cooks boil them as described above, but add a cup of cold water once the water comes to the boil. When the water returns to a boil again, another cup of cold water is added. This is repeated three or four times until the noodles are cooked.

Either way, you need to test the noodles frequently to make sure they don't overcook. A properly cooked noodle is slightly chewy and the same colour throughout. Once cooked, immediately drain and rinse the noodles in two or three cold-water baths or under cold running water. This stops them cooking and keeps the noodles from sticking together. If necessary, reheat by putting them in a colander and submerging in a pot of boiling water until just heated. Drain well and serve.

Noodles in Broth
Serves 2

This authentic Japanese dish is satisfying and quick to prepare. Noodles served in a clear broth like this recipe is a pretty standard lunch in Japan, with bars all over every city offering this dish. Try topping the noodles with a mix of steamed, simmered, or deep-fried vegetables and tofu for a complete dinner. Udon, brown rice udon, or soba are particularly recommended for this dish.

250g udon or soba noodles

2 tablespoons tamari or shoyu

½ tablespoon mirin

a pinch of sea salt

750ml dashi (page 48)

1-2 teaspoons juice squeezed from grated fresh ginger

2 spring onions, finely chopped

Cook the noodles as described above. Add the tamari or shoyu plus mirin and sea salt to the dashi, and simmer for 1 minute. Take the broth off the heat and add the ginger juice.

To serve, divide the noodles into two deep individual serving bowls. Ladle the hot broth over the noodles to almost cover them, and sprinkle with the chopped spring onion.

Spicy Soba Salad

Serves 3-4

Vary the vegetables according to seasonal availability. Fresh peas, sweetcorn, red and green peppers and radishes are all tasty and colourful variations for this dish.

250g soba

1 large or 2 medium carrots, cut into 4cm matchsticks

a head of broccoli cut into florets

2 spring onions, sliced

2 tablespoons fresh chopped parsley

Dressing:

2 tablespoons toasted sesame oil

¼ teaspoon chilli-flavoured sesame oil or a pinch of chilli powder

2 tablespoons tamari or shoyu

¼ teaspoon sea salt

3 tablespoons brown rice vinegar

1 clove garlic, finely chopped

Break noodles into even lengths of about a third, and boil them in about 2.5 litres of water, as described above. Steam the carrots and broccoli for a few minutes, then rinse under cold water. Combine all the vegetables with the cooked noodles in a medium-sized bowl. Whisk the dressing ingredients together in a cup with a fork, and add the liquid to the vegetables and noodles. Toss gently and serve.

Noodles With Miso-Tahini Sauce
Serves 2-3

Udon and lomein noodles go especially well with this popular sauce, and soba noodles taste good with it too. This version of the recipe is simply garnished with spring onions, but try topping the noodles and sauce with steamed vegetables.

250g uncooked udon or lomein

4 level tablespoons sweet white miso

3-4 tablespoons tahini

100ml cold water

2 tablespoons brown rice vinegar

1 tablespoon mirin

3cm fresh ginger root, grated and then squeezed for its juice

1 clove garlic, finely chopped

a pinch of dried tarragon, basil, or thyme

a finely chopped spring onion

Boil the noodles in 2.5 litres of water, as described above. Mix the miso and tahini in a small saucepan. Add the water a little at a time, and mix well to make a smooth sauce. Add the remaining ingredients and bring to a gentle simmer. If it's too thick, add a bit more water; if it's too thin, simmer briefly to thicken the sauce.

To serve, put the noodles into individual serving bowls, spoon the sauce over the top, and sprinkle with the spring onion.

Pickles & Condiments

Umeboshi Plums

Umeboshi Plums are salt-pickled Japanese plums, and Umeboshi Purée is a paste made from these plums. Umeboshi are one of the most amazingly delicious things you can imagine. The deep maroon-pink colour is offset by a rounded piquancy that's tart yet sweet, very salty and quite fruity all at the same time.

Umeboshi are made by pickling unripe Japanese ume plums with sea salt, then sun-drying and returning to the pickling juice. The vibrant pink colour of umeboshi comes from red shiso (perilla) leaves, which are pickled together with the ume. Red shiso is a mineral-rich herb, particularly high in iron. As well as giving umeboshi their beautiful colour, shiso adds minerals to the high vitamin C content of the ume. Umeboshi is available in three forms: whole plums pickled with or without shiso leaves, and umeboshi purée, made from pitted umeboshi.

Umeboshi don't just taste astonishingly good; they're also incredibly healthy according to Japanese folklore. They're soothing for all sorts of stomach problems. Umeboshi are also reported to help counteract fatigue, increase endurance, and stimulate the liver and kidneys to help dissolve and expel toxins. In this way, they help the body to purify the blood. It's these powerful antibacterial properties that also make umeboshi stop rice from going off, a fact used since ancient time to prevent food poisoning. Umeboshi's alkalinising effect make them a great general tonic. Added to rice porridge, umeboshi is the Japanese version of Jewish chicken soup. It's the cure-all food given by mums in Japan to sort out common colds and keep their families healthy.

There are lots of natural umeboshi producers in Japan, but few use the year-long traditional process of Cleaspring's two suppliers: the Sogawa family and the Morisho family. Hardly anyone uses organically grown plums and high-quality sea salt. In fact, most umeboshi are made in just a few weeks using red dye and industrial salt. To be sure you are buying finest-quality pickled plums, check the ingredients on the label. Clearspring Organic Umeboshi are made with organic plums, organic shiso leaves, sea salt... and nothing else.

Cooking with Umeboshi

Umeboshi plums and purée add zest to salad dressings, cooked vegetables, and sauces. They're also commonly served in Japan on the side with rice, in a bento box, or tucked inside a rice ball wrapped with nori. In summer, enjoy thick cucumber rounds spread thinly with umeboshi purée. Try spreading thinly on cooked sweet corn, or simply eat them on their own straight out of the jar.

Orange-Ume Dressing

Makes enough dressing for a salad for two

Try this refreshing summer dressing on green or noodle salads.

3 tablespoons sesame seeds

juice of half a lemon

juice of 1 ½ oranges

2 teaspoons umeboshi purée

1 teaspoon finely chopped spring onion or chives

2 tablespoons sesame or olive oil

Toast the sesame seeds in a dry frying pan over a medium heat for 2-3 minutes, stirring constantly with a wooden spoon. Pour them out of the pan and into your blender as soon as they're done. Add all of the other ingredients into the blender except the spring onion or chives, and blend until smooth. Mix the spring onion or chives in at the end, and chill for half an hour before serving.

Braised Cabbage with Umeboshi
Serves 3

½ a head of white or red cabbage

1 tablespoon toasted sesame oil

1½ tablespoons umeboshi paste or a chopped pitted umeboshi

Cut the cabbage half in half again lengthwise. Remove the hard stemmy core, and shred the leafy part thinly into ½ cm slices. Heat the oil over a medium heat in a frying pan, add the cabbage and sauté briefly, stirring with a wooden spoon. Add the umeboshi which at first won't mix evenly, but as you keep mixing, it will evenly coat the cabbage. Keep cooking like this for about 5 minutes.

After sautéing, if no juice has come out of the cabbage, add a very small drizzle of water, cover, lower the heat, and simmer over a low heat for 15-20 minutes, or until tender. Serve hot on the side with braised tofu or roasted buckwheat.

Takuan

Daikon is a long white Japanese radish sometimes found in good greengrocers and Asian stores. It has a slightly hot flavour, a bit like horseradish but smoother and milder. It's a staple vegetable in Japan, and is generally sold in the UK under its Chinese name, mooli.

Clearspring Takuan is simply daikon root pickled in rice bran, and is one of the most important and traditional of all Japanese pickles. Rich in B-vitamins and lactobacilli, takuan is still commonly made in rural Japanese homes every autumn and eaten throughout the winter. Clearspring Takuan is made with the same traditional farmhouse methods used for centuries, and contains no dyes or additives.

Serve it on the side with sushi and nori-maki, or try it in sandwiches instead of pickled gherkins. Also serve it up with oily dishes, like mackerel, as it's used in Japan to help digest fatty foods.

Sushi Ginger

Young, tender ginger roots are thinly sliced, briefly salt-pressed, then pickled in a vinegar mixture. They are called sushi ginger because they are almost always served with sushi or sashimi (raw fish). If you've ever been to a sushi bar, you've seen mounds of these paper-thin, pink or light brown pickles. Sushi ginger pickles can be served year-round as a digestive aid and taste complement with meals, especially those containing fish. They're particularly refreshing in summer.

Sushi ginger pickles available in oriental food stores and sushi bars nearly always contain sugar and dyes, and are almost certainly pickled in low-quality vinegar. Clearspring Sushi Ginger is unsweetened, and the colour comes from natural red shiso (perilla herb) leaves and its pickled in natural cider vinegar. It's excellent served with whole meals or as a snack straight out of the packet. And look out for sushi cucumber and sushi daikon, too.

Tekka

Tekka is an iron-rich, moist yet powdery condiment that's delicious sprinkled on grains, noodles, and vegetables. Clearspring Tekka is made by sautéing chopped burdock root, carrot, and lotus root in unrefined sesame oil, then adding Hatcho (soya bean) miso and cooking the mixture over a low heat for five to seven hours until crumbly and quite dry. Chopped ginger is added towards the end of cooking. Tekka should be used sparingly, since it's concentrated and strong. It's also known as miso condiment.

Shiso Condiment

Shiso condiment is known as *shiso momiji* in Japan. It is a healthier alternative to table salt, as it adds lots of minerals to your food along with it's salty taste. Its zesty, tart and salty flavour is especially good with grains and salads. Clearspring Shiso Condiment is made from iron-rich shiso (perilla herb) leaves, that are first pickled with umeboshi then sun-dried and powdered. Shiso condiment helps the body to maintain an alkaline condition, keeping you balanced.

Wasabi

Wasabi is the Japanese version of horseradish that's so strong it's nicknamed *namida* (tears) in Japanese. Although it's frequently compared to white horseradish, the two plants aren't related. Wasabi is a little less sharp, and is rounder and more aromatic than European horseradish. However, both have a similar kick.

Wasabi's biting freshness plus its variety of protein-digesting enzymes makes it a perfect complement to raw fish dishes like sashimi and sushi. It's also delicious inside vegetarian sushi. Mix a small amount of wasabi into the shoyu-seasoned dip to accompany sashimi. In preparing sushi, rub wasabi on bite-sized fingers of vinegared rice, then top with raw fish. Wasabi is also traditionally added to the broth or dipping sauce served with soba noodles.

Powdered wasabi keeps almost indefinitely if stored in a cool, dry place. Most commercial wasabi is actually horseradish with artificial green colouring added. When mixed with water to make a paste, it turns bright green, whereas authentic wasabi powder makes a duller green paste. Cleaspring Wasabi Powder has no artificial colours.

Preparing Wasabi

It is best to prepare only as much wasabi as you plan to use, because the flavour weakens over time. In a small cup mix one part water with two parts wasabi powder to make a paste. The paste should be thick, not runny. Cover the container, or turn it upside down on the counter and let it sit for about ten minutes to allow the flavour to heighten.

Avocado 'Sashimi'

Serves 6

Avocado's buttery texture and mild flavour are similar to some varieties of raw fish sashimi. As with sashimi, a dip of shoyu and wasabi is perfect served on the side. This appetiser works best as the first course of a dinner – its complex flavour awakens the taste buds.

1 small or medium-sized ripe avocado

the juice of a lemon

2 tablespoons shoyu

60ml cold water

1½ teaspoons wasabi powder

Halve the avocado lengthwise, slicing through to the stone. Twist halves and pull apart. Remove the pit, then peel the avocado. Thinly slice the avocado halves lengthwise, then coat the slices lightly with the lemon juice to stop them going brown. Put three slices onto each dish – sushi plates are ideal.

Mix the shoyu and water, dividing the mixture into individual dip saucers – allow about 1 tablespoon per serving. Add one drop of water at a time to the wasabi powder and mix until it forms a thick paste. Place a small dollop of wasabi on each plate of avocado "sashimi" for guests to mix into their shoyu dip. Try placing the wasabi on a very thin slice of red radish to add colour to this dish.

To eat, pick up each avocado slice with chopsticks, dip into the shoyu and wasabi, and enjoy. You can use this same dipping sauce for nori-maki rolls. These are small bundles of rice with thin strips of cucumber, avocado or carrot wrapped in nori.

Summer Soba
Serves 2

Cool and refreshing even when it's too hot to eat anything else, this traditional noodle dish is a favourite Japanese lunch on a hot summer day. Wasabi is also used to season hot noodles in broth, especially when soba noodles are used.

3 tablespoons tamari or shoyu

⅛ teaspoon sea salt

2 tablespoons mirin

750ml dashi (page 48)

200g uncooked soba

Condiments:

1 teaspoon wasabi powder

¼ sheet toasted nori, crumbled into bite-sized pieces

3 spring onions, finely chopped

Add the tamari or shoyu, and the mirin to the dashi in a medium sized saucepan. Simmer for a minute, remove from the heat, and leave to cool.

Boil the soba. Add one drop of water at a time to the wasabi and mix until it forms a thick paste. Get the other condiments ready. Divide the cooked noodles into small plates or soup bowls. If the noodles stick together, rinse them under cold water and drain well before serving.

Pour the chilled dipping broth into small individual bowls. Set out the prepared wasabi, nori and spring onions into separate bowls so they can be added to the broth to individual tastes. Dip each bite of noodles into the chilled broth. If the dip becomes weak, replace it with fresh broth.

Dried Tofu

Six times as concentrated as regular tofu, dried tofu has twice the protein of beef, fish and chicken, and none of the cholesterol. Dried tofu has a full complement of essential amino acids and is a concentrated source of iron, calcium and phosphorus. What's more, like other soya foods, dried tofu is an excellent source of isoflavones, known to help prevent some types of cancer and cardiovascular disease.

When shopping for dried tofu, be aware that industrial brands use bleaching agents and additives to make it pristine white and less brittle. Clearspring Dried Tofu is made with the highest quality non-GMO tofu and contains no additives or bleaching agents. It's simply tofu freeze-dried. Dried tofu keeps for several months, but gradually turns yellowy brown with age. Make sure that the dried tofu you buy is light brown, and store it in a cool, dry place away from direct sunlight.

Cooking with Dried Tofu

With its porous, firm yet tender texture and its mild, unimposing taste, dried tofu has an amazing ability to absorb flavours from foods and seasonings it is cooked with. It can be used in place of meat or poultry in Indian and Thai style curries, as well as in authentic Japanese dishes. Like a sponge, it's ready to pick up the flavour of seasonings, sauces, and marinades. It cooks in minutes and is delicious whether simmered, stewed, sautéed, or deep-fried.

Before dried tofu can be used, it has to be reconstituted. Simply soak the 5cm x 5cm pieces in warm water for five minutes, then press firmly between your hands. Keep soaking and pressing until the liquid that comes out is no longer milky.

Once reconstituted, there are three main ways to cook dried tofu. First, it can be diced and added to well-seasoned soups, stews, stir-fries or sauces. Secondly, try marinating it for thirty minutes in natural soya sauce, mirin, and ginger and then stir-fry for an authentic Japanese flavour. The third and most versatile method is to simmer the tofu in stock or miso soup. It can be served as it is, pan-fried in toasted sesame oil; or diced and added to stews, sautés, grains, sauces and salads. Simmered dried tofu is especially good deep-fried in tempura batter, or shallow fried dipped in egg and rolled in breadcrumbs. Try grating dried tofu whilst still dry and adding it to stuffing, casseroles, and burgers.

Hearty Winter Stew
Serves 3

Dried tofu is the concentrated source of protein in this classic winter one-pot meal. Serve with whole grain bread, brown rice or cous cous for a simple, warming and delicious dinner.

6 blocks of dried tofu

500ml dashi or vegetable stock

2 tablespoons tamari

1 tablespoon mirin

1 bay leaf

a pinch of rosemary

1 onion, cut into 8-12 wedges

3 carrots, cut into bite-sized chunks

1 stick of celery, cut on the diagonal into 5cm lengths

10-12 mushrooms, halved or quartered

3 x 2cm slices of winter squash, or 7 x 1cm slices of winter squash

12 broccoli florets

Soak the dried tofu in lukewarm water for 5 minutes. Repeatedly dampen the tofu and squeeze out excess water until the liquid that comes out is no longer milky. Cut tofu pieces in half lengthwise, then cut each of these halves into thirds.

In a large saucepan, bring half of the stock to a simmer with the tamari and mirin. Add the bay leaf, rosemary, onion, and tofu. Cover and simmer for 10 minutes. Add the remaining stock, carrots, celery, and mushrooms. Cover and simmer over a low heat for 5 minutes. Add the squash and simmer until the vegetables are nearly tender, which will be about 10 minutes. If the pan is nearly dry, add 100ml cold water mixed with 1 teaspoon shoyu. Add the broccoli and simmer for about 5 minutes, until tender but still a bit crunchy. Serve with whole grain bread, brown rice, cous cous or fried noodles for a simple warming dinner.

Mochi

Mochi comes as a hard block that, to be honest, doesn't look appetising. But when it is cooked, it goes golden and crispy on the outside and gorgeously gooey on the inside. Mochi is made from sticky rice known as sweet rice. Made the traditional way, whole sweet rice is soaked, steamed, and pounded. It's then allowed to dry until firm enough to slice.

Although mochi is still hand-pounded by Japanese home-cooks for special occasions like New Year, most of the bright white mochi found in Japanese supermarkets is made from highly refined sweet rice squeezed through a modern industrial food processor. Pounding sweet rice is back-breaking work, but mochi produced this way tastes far better than the industrial version. What's more, some traditionalists feel factory-extruded mochi lacks the healing qualities of the traditional pounded variety.

Fortunately, there are a few small mochi makers that combine the quality of pounding with the convenience of automation. One of these is Nobuyuki Kojima, maker of Clearspring's sweet brown rice mochi. Kojima's uniquely designed method of pounding sweet rice produces a high-energy mochi that tastes and feels just like the traditional thing.

Mochi is supremely versatile, and is generally served as the main ingredient of a meal. Naturally filling and slightly sweet, this rice food is also great on its own as a snack. Energising and easy to digest, mochi is an excellent food if you're feeling weak. Japanese farmers eat lots of mochi during winter because of its reputation for increasing stamina and warmth. Mochi is also traditionally included in the first meal of the Japanese New Year, usually in soup or stew, as it symbolises longevity and wealth.

According to traditional Japanese folk medicine, mochi is beneficial for anemia, blood-sugar imbalances, and weak intestines. It's also helpful for pregnant and lactating women, as it encourages a plentiful supply of breast milk. Mochi can also be made with added mugwort, a herb that grows wild throughout Japan. Mochi with added mugwort taste deep, earthy and very savoury.

Cooking With Mochi

Mochi is really easy to cook. It can be baked, grilled, pan-fried, or deep-fried. When cooked, mochi puffs up to nearly double its original size, developing a crisp crust outside and a soft, melting interior. If cooked too long, the surface cracks and the soft part inside oozes out, so watch mochi carefully while it cooks.

Baked or grilled mochi is often eaten with a sweet miso topping. Baked mochi can also be cut into bite-sized pieces and added to soups during the last minute of cooking. Pan or deep-fried mochi doesn't need anything more than a squirt of soya sauce or a soya sauce and fresh ginger dip. Mochi can also be rolled in rice syrup, then coated with ground walnuts and eaten as dessert. For the ultimate quick and easy snack, shallow frying a couple of pieces of mochi, then rolling the hot and squidgy rectangles in toasted nori smeared with grated ginger, tamari, tekka and wasabi... Heaven and whole grain!

The recipe for mochi soup also contains fresh burdock root. The best way to make sure you can get burdock root in the UK is to grow your own. Failing that, try specialist organic stores, or Japanese food shops.

Mochi Soup (*Ozōni*)
Serves 5-6

1 burdock root

1 large carrot

2 litres dashi (page 48)

½ teaspoon sea salt

6 dried shiitake or maitake, soaked and sliced

1 tablespoon mirin

3 spring onions, trimmed and cut into 2cm lengths

4 Chinese cabbage leaves, chopped

6 pieces mochi

4 tablespoons white miso or 2 tablespoons shoyu soya sauce

Scrub the burdock, cut into 5cm julienne strips, and place in cold water to prevent discoloration. Cut the carrot in a similar way, but a bit thicker. Drain the burdock and add it to the dashi in a saucepan. Simmer for 15 minutes over a medium heat, then add the carrots and mushrooms. Simmer for 10 more minutes.

Add the mirin, spring onions and cabbage leaves, and cook for 5 more minutes. While the soup is cooking, place the mochi onto a lightly oiled baking sheet. Bake at 180°C / Gas Mark 4 until slightly brown and puffy. Check regularly to see if it's done. It will take about ten minutes. When they're ready, take the mochi out of the oven, and cut into bite-sized pieces.

When the cabbage is just tender, add the mochi and gently simmer for 1 more minute. If you're using shoyu, now's the time to add it. If you're using miso, dissolve the miso paste in a little bit of the broth before adding it to the soup. Let the soup sit for a couple of minutes before serving.

Deep-Fried Mochi in Broth
Serves 3

Deep-fried mochi is delicious when served with a dip or wrapped in toasted nori strips, but see if you can resist eating it before it gets into this soup!

3 tablespoons shoyu

2 tablespoons mirin

½ litre dashi (page 48)

sunflower oil for deep-frying

9 pieces mochi

50g finely grated daikon

3 spring onions, finely chopped

Add the shoyu and mirin to the dashi, and simmer briefly, being careful not to let it boil.

In a saucepan, heat 5cm depth of oil to about 170°C. This is the temperature at which a drop of flour and water batter will sink to the bottom of the pan and immediately rise back up to the surface. Gently place mochi, 2 to 3 pieces at a time, into oil and fry, turning occasionally until the outside is crisp and golden. Drain on kitchen paper. Continue until all the mochi pieces are fried.

Put three pieces of mochi into each individual serving bowl. Pour a third of the hot dashi broth over each plate of mochi, and top with the grated daikon and spring onions.

Maitake

Mushrooms

Mushrooms are treasured throughout the East for maintaining health, curing disease, and promoting vitality. Maitake are considered the king of mushrooms, because they are so delicious and have a reputation as a powerful healing food. Maitake literally means 'dancing mushroom' in Japanese, because people who found them deep in the mountains danced for joy.

In the past twenty years, medical researchers have been studying the anti-tumour activity of many types of mushrooms. Most medicinal mushrooms, such as maitake, reishi and shiitake, enhance immune function by stimulating cell-mediated immunity. Simply put, they can turn on the immune system's T-cells, which travel the bloodstream seeking and destroying cancer cells. As such, continuing research is going on in the USA and Japan into how mushrooms like maitake could be used to treat and prevent cancer and HIV, plus diabetes and even obesity. No wonder maitake are called dancing mushrooms!

All maitake are not the same. Although wild maitake still exist deep in some forests, almost all maitake used for food and medicine are cultivated. Like other medicinal and culinary plants, the quality of maitake depends on growing conditions and genetic constitution. Through the years, scientists have learned that maitake produce the most potent medicinal effects and have the best flavour when the highest quality of spores are used for cultivation under ideal growing conditions.

Clearspring Maitake are grown by Yukiguni in Nigata Prefecture. Yukiguni maitake are not only served fresh in Japan's best restaurants, but their high potency extract is the first choice of medical researchers around the world.

Cooking with Dried Maitake

Whole dried maitake offer medicinal benefits as a side dish to the succulent, distinctive flavour that makes them a prized gourmet mushroom. Slow drying concentrates their rich taste and medicinal qualities ready for use throughout the year. Soak dried maitake in lukewarm water for twenty minutes and use them with their soaking water to make superb soups or sauces. Alternatively, soak them and add to stir-fries, fried rice or noodles, or casseroles.

Spring Tonic Miso Soup with Maitake

Serves 4

This soup is a delicious way to give your immune system a boost. Substitute other spring vegetables if you want, and cook until tender.

7g dried maitake mushrooms

1¼ litres cold water

300g fresh tofu, cut into 1cm cubes

100g watercress, chopped into 5cm lengths

3 tablespoons brown rice or barley miso

4 spring onions, cut into thin slices

Soak the maitake in the water in a saucepan for 15-20 minutes. Bring the water and mushrooms to a simmer over a medium heat, and gently cook the maitake for 15 minutes. Add tofu and simmer for about a minute, then add the watercress and simmer another minute or so. Take the soup off the heat. In a cup, dissolve the miso in a little bit of the liquid, and add it to the soup. Sprinkle with the spring onions and serve.

Vegetable Barley Stew

Serves 6

Rice or barley stews seasoned with miso or umeboshi are the Japanese mother's cure-all. Maitake adds its healing and rejuvenating qualities to make this an even healthier dish. Enjoy this creamy, soothing stew any time during the colder months, especially if you're feeling weak or out of balance. And make plenty – this dish tastes best a day or two after it's made.

200g barley

10g dried maitake

3 litres water

15cm piece kombu

1 teaspoon sea salt

1 bay leaf

½ teaspoon oregano

1 onion, diced

1 leek, sliced

2 large carrots, cut in half lengthwise, then into ½ cm thick half moons

a stick of celery, sliced

150g chopped kale or other leafy greens, such as chard or Savoy cabbage

2-3 tablespoons brown rice or barley miso, to taste

chopped fresh parsley or sliced spring onion

Wash the barley and put in a large saucepan with the maitake, water, and kombu. Use a small plate or bowl to keep mushrooms submerged, and soak for 1-3 hours. Take the kombu out, and keep it for another time. Remove the maitake, chop them finely, and put them back in the pan.

Bring the liquid to the boil over a medium heat, and add salt and a bay leaf. Lower the heat and simmer with the lid on but ajar, until the barley is tender. This will be about 45 minutes, or an extra 20 minutes or so for a creamier texture.

Add oregano and all the vegetables except the greens. Simmer 10 minutes. Add kale and simmer for 15 minutes more. Remove from heat. In a cup, dilute the miso in a little bit of hot water, and add it to the stew. Sprinkle with chopped parsley or spring onion, and serve hot.

Shiitake

Mushrooms

Shiitake are Japanese forest mushrooms. Long prized by the Japanese for their distinctive taste and natural goodness, they are simply loaded with nutrition. They contain all eight essential amino acids and are a good source of B vitamins. Worldwide attention is now being given to shiitake's medicinal properties. Scientists have recently isolated substances from shiitake that may play a role in the cure and prevention of heart disease, cancer and AIDS.

Clearspring Shiitake are traditionally grown on *shii* (oak) logs in the humid forests of southern Japan, then hand-harvested at their peak of vitality. The harvesting time is very important. If the mushrooms are left on the log too long, they will completely open and shed their spores, producing mushrooms that are flat, dark and lacking in vitality. After harvest Clearspring shiitake are carefully sun-dried to concentrate and preserve their woody, meaty flavour and goodness for year-round use.

By contrast to this traditional Japanese process, most fresh shiitake in stores today are grown on sawdust blocks in a temperature controlled environment, never seeing the light of day.

Cooking with Shiitake

Cover the mushrooms in lukewarm water for at least 30 minutes. Once rehydrated, remove and discard any stems and thinly slice the caps. Use with their soaking water for superb soups, stews and sauces, or add the sliced mushrooms to stir-fries, fried rice or noodles, or casseroles.

Shiitake Gravy

makes a 500ml jug of gravy

Pour this tasty gravy liberally all over your favourite grain dishes and roasts.

2 tablespoons extra virgin olive oil

2 shiitake, soaked and sliced (reserve 500ml soaking water)

1 small onion, diced

2 cloves garlic, chopped

3 tablespoons wheat flour

1 tablespoon shoyu

½ teaspoon dried thyme

1 tablespoon mirin or white wine

Heat the oil in a small frying pan and sauté the shiitake, onion and garlic over a medium-low heat for about 5 minutes, until the onion is translucent. Lower the heat, sprinkle the flour over the vegetables, and stir constantly for 2-3 minutes.

Slowly add the soaking water while stirring with a wooden spoon to stop the flour from going lumpy. Keep stirring until the gravy begins to simmer and thicken. Add the shoyu, thyme and mirin or wine, and simmer gently for about 15 minutes, stirring now and then. Keep warm until you're ready to serve.

Shiitake Tea

This is a traditional folk remedy to relax and soothe fevers.

To prepare, soak one mushroom for an hour, then cut it into quarters and bring it to a simmer with 500ml of soaking water or fresh water. Simmer for 10-20 minutes, or until the liquid has reduced by half. Add a dash of shoyu, then drink half a cup at a time. Also try adding 5g dried daikon to the pan for a more stimulating remedy.

Lotus Root

Lotus root gets the prize for being the most outlandish vegetable you can buy. It has little tunnels running the length of each root which when sliced make a pretty pattern. The lotus is an exotic plant that grows in muddy ponds or paddies in sub-tropical climates. The roots that we eat are actually called rhizomes. They form fat links planted in the mud under water. New leaves emerge from them, the stems elongating so that the first two or three leaves float on top of the water. The stem continues to grow, and subsequent leaves stand above the water. The fragrant pink or white flowers bloom in late summer, and they're gorgeous.

The rhizome, or root of the lotus, has been considered a delicacy in oriental cooking for over a thousand years. Its mild flavour goes well with most other vegetables, and its crunchy texture is great in stir-fries or served thinly sliced and deep-fried with or without batter.

Every part of the lotus plant is used in oriental medicine – seeds, leaves and flowers, as well as the root. Though the entire rhizome can be used medicinally, the part where the links join has the greatest effect. Small doses of lotus root juice are prescribed by naturopaths for lung-related ailments such as tuberculosis, asthma, and coughing, for heart disease, and to increase energy and neutralise toxins. Tea made from the grated and dried root is also used for these conditions.

As fresh lotus root is difficult to find, lotus root dishes, or *renkon* in Japanese, are usually prepared from dried sliced roots. Clearspring's dried lotus root slices are unbleached, making them darker in colour than most dried lotus root available.

Cooking with Dried Lotus Root

Dried lotus root is easy to use. Simply soak for two hours, then drain. This exotic vegetable can then be sautéed, steamed or simmered.

Stir-fried Vegetables with Pickled Plum Sauce

Serves 4

10cm strip of kombu

250ml of water

1½ tablespoons umeboshi paste

a pinch of sea salt

1 tablespoon mirin

half a head of Chinese cabbage

1 red pepper

20 snow peas or mangetout

50g dried lotus root, soaked for 2 hours

3-4 spring onions, cut into 2cm lengths

10g kuzu, crushed to a powder

Put the kombu and water in a small saucepan, bring to a simmer, uncovered, over a medium heat, then simmer gently for 5 minutes. Remove the kombu and keep it to use another time. Add the umeboshi, salt and mirin to this kombu stock and mix well, leaving it ready for later.

Next, cut the Chinese cabbage half in half again lengthwise, then core it and slice the leaves crosswise into 2cm wide strips. The core can be used if very thinly sliced. Quarter the red pepper, remove and discard seeds and inner white membranes, then thinly slice on the diagonal. Top and tail the snow peas or mangetout, removing any stringy bits.

Heat the oil over a medium heat in a wok or big frying pan. Drain the lotus root and sauté it briefly. Add the red pepper, then the Chinese cabbage, then the spring onions, sautéing for one minute after each vegetable is added. Lower the heat, cover and simmer for 5 minutes. Add the snow peas or mangetout, toss, cover and cook for one more minute. Uncover and remove from the heat.

Dissolve the kuzu in 30ml cold water and add to the kombu stock. Pour the stock over the vegetables and bring to the boil over a medium heat, stirring gently. Simmer for 1-2 minutes or until the sauce thickens. Serve as a vegetable dish on its own, or as a topping for noodles.

Agar-Agar

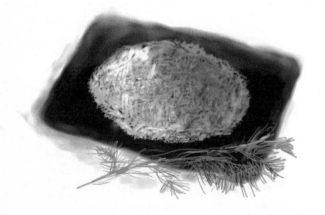

Agar-agar (*kanten*) is made from sea vegetables, and is used as a gelling agent to replace gelatine in jellies. Agar-agar's natural gelling ability, mild flavour, and total lack of calories have made it a favourite with health-conscious and vegetarian cooks around the world. Even at room temperature, it sets quickly as it cools, and seals in the natural flavour and sweetness of any fruits and vegetables used. And it has the benefit of a naturally high fibre content.

Light and refreshingly cool, agar-agar dishes are especially popular in the summer, but it can be used with vegetables and stock to make beautiful moulded aspics any time of the year. Not only are these translucent jellies a top way to get children excited about vegetables, they're real show-stoppers for dinner parties. Try using it as a substitute for pectin in jams, jellies, and cranberry sauce, and in puddings and pie fillings.

Today, almost all agar-agar is made by a modern process involving the use of sulphuric acid to dissolve the starches, and chemical bleaches and dyes to neutralise the colour and flavour. However, a few small producers, such as the Mizoguchi family in the mountains of Nagano, Japan, maker of Clearspring Agar-agar Flakes, still use the old labour-intense traditional method.

The natural snow-dried method begins on Japan's coast, where specific varieties of red sea vegetables are harvested and sun-dried. These are bundled and taken up to the Mizoguchi shop to be made into agar-agar during the winter months.

Beginning in December, the sea vegetables are placed in a large cauldron with water and allowed to cook down for several hours. The resulting gel is left to cool. It is then cut into blocks, arranged on bamboo trays, and set outside on snow-covered rice paddies. Moisture in the gelatine freezes each night then thaws during the day. In about ten days, all the moisture is gone and the light, flaky bars of pure agar-agar remain. The crisp, porous, feather-light bars are then shaved into fine flakes and packaged.

Cooking with Agar-Agar Flakes

Simply measure your agar-agar flakes and sprinkle them over the liquid before heating. Bring to a simmer over a medium heat without stirring. Simmer for three to five minutes, stirring occasionally, until the flakes dissolve. Agar-agar flakes set quickly as it cools, sealing in the natural flavours.

One slightly rounded tablespoon of agar-agar flakes will gel roughly one cup of liquid. Acidic foods may need a bit more agar-agar than alkaline foods. Test each recipe by taking a spoonful of the heated mixture and dropping it on a cold plate. If the mixture doesn't set in a few minutes, sprinkle a few more agar-agar flakes into the pot and simmer for a few more minutes.

Apple-Berry Cooler
Serves 6

1 litre apple or apple-strawberry juice

a small pinch of sea salt

4 slightly rounded tablespoons agar-agar flakes

a 250g punnet of fresh berries, such as raspberries, strawberries, etc

Pour the juice into a small saucepan and add the salt. Sprinkle the agar-agar flakes on top, and bring to a gentle simmer over a medium heat without stirring. Once the liquid begins to simmer, gently stir it now and then with a wooden spoon. Simmer for 3 minutes, then remove from the heat.

Pour over the whole or sliced berries in a mould or a bowl. When it's cooled down a bit, put the bowl in the fridge. It'll be firm in about 1-2 hours. Then either scoop out spoonfuls, or turn out the whole jelly by gently pulling the sides of the jelly away from the mould, and inverting the dish over a plate.

Apple-Sesame Custard*

Serves 6-8

Served chilled, this is a refreshing summer dessert.

1½ litres apple juice

a pinch of sea salt

15g agar-agar flakes

3 tablespoons finely grated lemon peel

5 tablespoons tahini

a whole vanilla pod or a few drops of vanilla essence

Put the apple juice, agar-agar flakes and lemon peel into a medium saucepan, and leave to soak for 10-15 minutes. Add the salt, bring the mixture to a boil, then lower the heat, and simmer 3-5 minutes. Stir every now and then with a wooden spoon until the agar-agar flakes have completely dissolved. Then remove from the heat.

Put the tahini into a small bowl. Gradually add about 100ml of hot juice, stirring as you add it. When the tahini reaches a thin, creamy consistency, add it to the pot and stir it in. Slice the vanilla pod along its length, and scrape out the seeds. Mix this seedy paste into the custard.

Rinse a shallow bowl or casserole dish in water, then pour in the hot liquid. Leave to cool until it's firm. This will take a couple of hours. Purée the mixture in a blender until smooth. Leave the custard in a bowl in the fridge, then serve either on its own or as a topping for other desserts, like apple crumble.

Summary Pudding*
Serves 4

This is a delightful variation on the classic English dessert.

2 cups blackberries (or other berries)

4 apples

3 teaspoons sultanas

4-6 slices of brown bread

1 tablespoon orange zest

3 tablespoons agar-agar flakes

2 tablespoons malt syrup

a pinch of sea salt

2 tablespoons apple juice concentrate

carob spread

cinnamon powder

custard or soya dessert topping

Core, peel and dice the apples. Place the diced apple, sultanas, pinch of sea salt and cinnamon in a saucepan, adding water to cover only one third of the volume of the fruit. Cover and cook for 10-15 minutes. Add the agar-agar flakes, berries, malt syrup and apple juice concentrate to taste. Simmer uncovered for 10 more minutes. Stir in the orange zest.

Spread some carob spread on each slice of bread. Line a pudding basin with the bread slices, keeping the spread side facing inwards and holding a slice or two back for covering the top. Fill the lined basin with the cooked fruit. Cover the top with the rest of the bread. Place a weighted saucer or plate on top of the pudding then leave to cool and set. Turn out and unfold. Serve with your choice of custard or soya dessert.

Kuzu

Wild Mountain Root Starch

Pure white chunks of Kuzu starch are extracted from the root of a legume plant that has been part of Chinese and Japanese cuisine for more than two thousand years. It's very high in complex starch molecules, so its main use is as a powerful thickening agent.

So why not just use cornflour to thicken your sauces? Because whilst cornflour can do much the same job, it is highly processed and treated with chemical bleaches and extracting agents, whereas kuzu is a seriously healing food. It can help relieve many digestive complaints, including excess acidity, stomach aches, bacterial infections, and diarrhoea.

Roots are a focal point of a plant's energy. They have always had a special place in both our diet and herbal medicine. Ginseng, dock, radish, beetroot and carrots are all prized for their concentrated food value and healing powers. Averaging 200 pounds, kuzu is one of the world's largest vegetable roots, and is big business for Japanese and Chinese medicine.

Clearspring Traditional Organic Kuzu is made by Hirohachido Company located at the edge of Kagoshima Bay in southern Kyushu. The labour-intensive four-month process of separating the starch from the fibrous kuzu root starts when the roots are cleaned, then cut, mashed, and washed repeatedly in cold water to produce a crude paste. This paste is then repeatedly washed and filtered through silk screens to remove plant fibres and bitter tannins.

After settling, the kuzu paste is redissolved in cold water and filtered again. The washing, filtering, and settling process continues until a pure white, clay-like starch is formed. The starch is cut into 25cm thick blocks and placed in paper-lined boxes to dry for about sixty days. When properly dried, each block of kuzu is crumbled, and packaged.

Sweet potato starch can be extracted in just three or four days with twice as much yield as kuzu. Most kuzu manufacturers understandably mix potato starch with their kuzu powder to cut costs. However, Clearspring traditionally-made organic kuzu is 100% kuzu.

When you open your jar, you'll see the kuzu isn't powdered, but is in uneven chunks that look a bit like chalk. You can simply powder kuzu by crushing with the back of a spoon on a hard surface, or you can use a traditional Japanese suribachi and surikogi, which Clearspring import to the UK. A suribachi is a medium-sized pottery bowl with a rough inside surface. A surikogi is a wooden pestle. You use this pair like a pestle and mortar, but because the suribachi has a rough inner surface, it grinds a lot more effectively. You can also use a suribachi to purée miso and grind other spices and herbs, sea salt, garlic cloves, and anything else that needs an extra-effective pestle and mortar.

Kuzu Remedies

Kuzu root starch remedies can be used to treat minor indigestion, colds and minor aches and pains. Eating foods made with kuzu can have the same effect, and is considered good preventive medicine in Japan and China.

In his book Healing Ourselves (Avon Books, 1973), holistic health practitioner Naboru Muramoto recommends a drink called kuzu cream (see recipe page136) for colds, general body pains, stomach cramps, and diarrhoea. Kuzu cream is also recommended for neutralising stomach acidity and for relaxing tight muscles. When made with added ginger juice and chopped umeboshi, the drink is especially potent, plus tastes amazing. The ginger aids digestion and circulation while the salt plum neutralises lactic acid and eliminates it from the body.

Alternatively, simply use kuzu in cooking to thicken sauces, and enjoy its preventative effect whilst tucking into delicious dinners.

Carrots in Ginger Sauce
Serves 3

Carrots never tasted so good...

2 teaspoons toasted sesame oil

3 carrots, cut into thin diagonal slices

a pinch of sea salt

250ml cold water

1 large handful chopped parsley or watercress

1 teaspoon shoyu

10g kuzu,

1½ - 2 teaspoons of juice squeezed from fresh grated ginger root

Heat the oil in a frying pan, add the carrots, and mix with a wooden spoon. Sauté for about 3-5 minutes. Add the water, salt, cover, and simmer over a low heat for 5-10 minutes, until the carrots are just tender. Add greens and shoyu, mix together, and simmer for a couple more minutes. Take the pan off the heat.

Dissolve the kuzu in a tablespoon of cold water, and slowly add it to the vegetables while stirring constantly. Put the pan back on the heat, and bring to a simmer while you continue to stir. Cook for another couple of minutes, then add the freshly squeezed ginger juice. Mix and serve as a side dish.

Kuzu Fruit Custard

Makes about 3 cups

This light fruit dessert is delicious when eaten on its own. It can also be used to dress up other simple desserts. It makes a great topping for puddings, pies or tarts, especially vanilla ones. It also makes an excellent filling for pancakes.

250ml apple juice

¼ - ⅓ jar brown rice malt syrup, to taste

250 - 400g sliced pitted soft fruit e.g. apricots, peaches, nectarines, cherries

2 tablespoons kuzu

a pinch of sea salt

Mix the juice, malt syrup and pinch of sea salt in a saucepan. Adjust the amount of syrup you're using depending on the sweetness or tartness of the fruit.

If you're using large fruit like nectarines, cut it into bite-sized pieces. If the fruit you're using is fairly firm, add it to the pan and bring to a simmer, uncovered, over a medium heat for a couple of minutes. Delicate, tender fruits won't need to be cooked, so leave them in your serving bowl until later.

Thoroughly dissolve the kuzu in 2 tablespoons cool water and add to the pan while stirring it quickly. Cook on a medium to low heat and stir constantly until the mixture gets back up to a simmer and thickens.

If you're using fruit that doesn't need cooking, pour the hot liquid over it at this stage. Mix gently and once it's cooled down, put it in the fridge. If the fruit's already mixed in, simply pour the contents of the pan into the serving bowl, leave to cool and put it into the fridge. The custard will thicken as it cools.

Stomach-Settling Kuzu Cream
Serves 1

If you're making this to treat digestive discomfort, drink it about one hour before a meal to get the maximum effect. Serve the cream warm, but allow it to cool for one minute after you prepare it. This recipe makes a thick, pudding-like cream. If you'd prefer to make a thinner drink, reduce the amount of kuzu to one rounded teaspoon.

1½ (15g) tablespoons kuzu
1 umeboshi plum, pitted and finely chopped or 1 teaspoon umeboshi paste
¼ - ½ teaspoon of juice squeezed from freshly grated ginger root
a dash of shoyu soya sauce

In a small saucepan, thoroughly dissolve kuzu in 250ml cold water. Add the umeboshi and simmer over a medium heat, stirring frequently with a wooden spoon. As soon as the mixture begins to bubble around the edges, stir constantly until the kuzu thickens and becomes translucent. Gently simmer for a couple of minutes, then remove from the heat. Squeeze the freshly grated ginger over the pan to add fresh ginger juice. Discard the ginger pulp, and add shoyu to taste.

Japanese Teas

Sencha, hojicha and *kukicha* are Japan's most popular teas. Mildly stimulating and slightly aromatic, these gentle teas are refreshing whilst being low in caffeine, and perfectly heighten the pleasure of Japanese cuisine.

Buddhist monks from ancient China originally brought tea (*cha*) to Japan where for centuries it was a rare and expensive commodity. After generations of experimentation and cultivation, tea is now Japan's national drink. From *Cha-no-yu*, the Zen Buddhist tea ceremony, to *o-cha*, the daily three o'clock tea break, drinking tea is a Japanese institution even beyond the British obsession.

Japan's finest teas are grown around the town of Uji, which is located on the old road between the ancient capitals of Nara and Kyoto. Uji's rich, slightly acidic soil is ideal for growing tea. Early morning mist from the Uji River moistens the leaves of the plants, shielding them from the sun. Following the natural contours of the valleys and surrounding hills, Uji's landscape is patched with three and four-acre tea fields. Straight rows of smooth, tightly trimmed bushes look more like ornamental hedges than individual tea plants.

Off the main road, on a hill overlooking Uji, the manicured look of the plantations below gives way to fields of lumpy, irregular rows of tea plants - the remote, centuries-old tea plantation of the Nagata family, producers of Clearspring Organic Sencha, Hojicha, Kukicha and Genmaicha Teas. Following the principles of an agricultural method known in Japan as 'nature farming', the Nagatas have become a local curiosity to their tea-farming neighbours. Most tea farmers spray their plants with industrial pesticides and herbicides fifteen to twenty times a year, but the Nagata family never uses chemicals. They also don't use animal manures, replenishing the nutrients in their topsoil using only vegetable compost. Nature farming stresses the importance of building soil vitality by maintaining a semi-wild natural environment. Plants are not overly protected or pampered but are allowed to fend for themselves with the help of a strong, balanced soil.

In spring, one of the first pickings of the delicate, aromatic tea leaves is for sencha, Japan's high quality leaf green tea. A special steaming process enhances and protects the bright colour of this tea. Enzymes in each leaf would naturally turn the leaves dark, but steaming stops this process. Although most English, Chinese, and Indian teas come from the same type of tea bush, they are not steamed, turning the dark brown colour that we know as black tea.

Recent research has confirmed what Eastern healers have long known. Green tea's traditional steaming process is partly responsible for its extraordinary healing properties. Scientists working in the USA and Japan have found that drinking green tea may not only help to prevent heart disease and strokes, but may also reduce the risk of many types of cancer, regulate blood sugar, lower blood pressure, boost the immune system, facilitate weight loss, help prevent ulcers, slow the aging process, fight viral colds and flu, and even prevent gum disease, cavities and bad breath. Many of these possible health benefits come from green tea's rich supply of polyphenols, which are one of nature's most powerful antioxidants. Even though black tea and green tea come from the same kind of tea bush, black teas lose a lot of their health promoting properties during fermentation. Research has shown green tea has six times the antioxidant capability of black fermented teas.

After the young, tender leaves have been picked and processed into sencha, mature leaves and small twigs are gathered to make hojicha, or roasted green tea. Hojicha is the tea usually served in Japanese restaurants, because it goes well with food and is also less expensive. Hojicha contains less caffeine than other green teas, so it's better for children or for your bedtime cuppa. Since the leaves are carefully roasted to make hojicha, it has a robust, smoky taste that is quite different from the slightly tart taste of sencha. Most green teas become bitter when cooled, but hojicha makes an excellent and refreshing iced tea.

The final tea cutting is called kukicha, or roasted twig tea. It's made from twigs and stems from the same bush, but is not classed as a green tea. The twigs and stems are steamed, dried and left to age for two to three years to develop the best flavour. Then they are roasted different lengths of time according to size. Kukicha contains few leaves, so it's very low in caffeine. Unlike green teas, which are always infused either in a teapot or in the cup, loose kukicha is usually boiled in a pan with hot water. It has a delicate, earthy and slightly roasted flavour. Like hojicha, kukicha can be served as iced tea, and is great mixed with apple juice for children. Kukicha and hojicha can also be mixed with shoyu, umeboshi, ginger, and kuzu to make traditional healing drinks.

Genmaicha literally means brown rice tea, and is a blend of green tea (sencha) and roasted brown rice. It's mild and refreshing like green tea, but has an added nutty flavour and aroma because of the brown rice in it.

Tea Preparation

In Japan, making tea is recognised as an art. For the average Westerner, there are three main elements to pay attention to: perfect water temperature, an eye to the clock when brewing, and using a porcelain or earthenware pot. If the water is too hot, the delicate taste of green tea can be destroyed, so use water off the boil. If brewed too long, green tea can easily stew, becoming dark and bitter.

Japanese tea is never served with milk or sugar, although a little rice syrup can be added for sweetness. Sencha is usually served after meals, whereas all the others can accompany food. Kukicha should be simmered for at least five minutes to bring out its full flavour. Try adding half an umeboshi plum plus a dash of shoyu to a cup of kukicha for a great hangover cure, too!

Brown Rice Malt Syrup

Brown rice malt syrup has a full, slightly nutty flavour with a hint of butterscotch. Its gentle, balanced sweetness is the perfect alternative to sugar, honey or maple syrup. Although honey and maple syrup do contain some vitamins and minerals, they are high in simple sugars. These are substances like glucose that are absorbed very quickly into the blood stream, but leave you feeling disoriented and depleted of energy soon after the sugar high.

Clearspring's Japanese Brown Rice Malt Syrup contains about 30% soluble complex carbohydrates, 45% maltose (grain-malt sugar), 5% glucose, and 20% water. The glucose is absorbed into the blood almost immediately. The maltose takes up to one and a half hours to digest, and the complex carbohydrates are gradually digested and released for up to four hours. Unlike cane sugar, honey and maple syrup, rice malt provides a slow and prolonged source of energy that is calming and soothing.

Like many traditional Japanese foods, brown rice malt syrup is made by a slow, natural enzymatic process. As the whole rice grains are partially broken down, they ooze a thick, richly flavoured, sweet liquid. Brown rice malt syrup contains many of the B vitamins and minerals found in whole rice and sprouted barley.

Making brown rice malt syrup is a complex craft requiring a great deal of labour, knowledge, and fine-tuned intuition. Japan's only remaining authentic brown rice syrup producer is the Uchida Toka Company in Fukuyama. These are the makers of Clearspring Brown Rice Malt Syrup, and also the brown rice syrup used in the Clearspring range of Sweet Rice Candies.

Cooking with Brown Rice Malt Syrup

Characteristically rich but mild flavoured, brown rice malt syrup is perhaps better in simple foods than honey, maple syrup, and molasses, as they have stronger, often overpowering tastes. As well as being a top option for biscuits, cakes and desserts, brown rice malt syrup is excellent in salad dressings and dips, as well as in vegetable dishes such as candied yams and pickles. All Clearspring malt syrups are a lot less sweet than sugar, honey, and maple syrup. To get your recipes up to the equivalent sweetness, substitute one and a half times the amount of rice syrup to white sugar. When substituting rice malt syrup for sugar, reduce the total amount of liquid that is called for in the recipe.

Apple and Blackberry Pie
Makes a 20cm pie

Nothing makes an autumn home happy like a homemade fruit pie. This one is extra quick and easy to make.

For the filling:
250g punnet of blackberries, washed
2-3 apples, cored and thinly sliced
200ml brown rice malt syrup
100g granulated tapioca

For the pastry:
175g plain flour
100ml sesame oil
2 tablespoons brown rice malt syrup
a little cold water

Pre-heat the oven to 190°C/ Gas Mark 5. To make the pie crust, rub the oil into the flour to form crumbs, either by hand or using a food processor. Mix in the brown rice malt syrup with a little cold water to bind the mixture. Wrap the pastry in cling film and put it in the fridge for about ten minutes.

Meanwhile, make the filling by gently mixing the blackberries, rice malt syrup and tapioca in a medium sized bowl. Pour over the sliced apples, and set aside.

Next, flour a work surface, and roll out the pastry using a well floured rolling pin. Transfer half of the pastry into a well-oiled 20cm pie dish, using your rolling pin. Pour the fruit mixture in. Cover with the rest of the pastry and trim, leaving about 1cm of crust overhanging the rim of the dish. Fold the top crust under the bottom crust and seal the pie by pressing around the edge with the back of a fork. Prick the top crust with the fork to make a few holes, allowing steam to escape.

Bake for 50-60 minutes. Leave the pie in the dish to cool thoroughly. Serve it with cold amazake or apple sesame custard.

Plum Sorbet

Makes about half a litre

This is a very simple and pretty dessert. Although plums are not as commonly used in frozen desserts as peaches, berries, and citrus fruits, they make an especially lush and creamy sorbet.

6 soft, ripe plums, halved and pitted

80ml water

1½ teaspoons agar-agar flakes

about 200g brown rice malt syrup, to taste

juice of half a small lemon

Put the plums and water into a small saucepan, and bring to a simmer. Put the lid on, and cook gently over medium-low heat, stirring now and then with a wooden spoon until they're tender. This will be about 10-15 minutes. Take the pan off the heat. With a slotted spoon, fish out the plums, and put them into a blender or food processor.

Sprinkle the agar-agar flakes over the remaining cooking liquid and gently simmer for 3 minutes, stirring occasionally. Add the liquid to the blender and purée until smooth. While the plums are still hot, add the syrup and lemon juice, and mix well. Pour the mixture into a plastic tub, and freeze for at least 6 hours, until solid.

This plum sorbet is smooth enough to scoop out and eat as it is at this stage of the recipe. For a smoother texture, blend the sorbet again a few hours before you serve it. Scrape the frozen mixture up with a fork until it looks like finely crushed ice. Spoon half of it into a blender and blend until it's light and smooth. Make sure you do it quickly so the sorbet doesn't thaw. Blend the other half in the same way. Place the blended sorbet back into the plastic tub, cover, and freeze until it's firm again. This will take about 1-3 hours. You could also try freezing the sorbet in an ice cube tray instead of the plastic tub to make instant kid-sized servings.

Amazake

Amazake (pronounced ah-mah-zah-kay) is unlike any other food you've come across. It's sweet without sugar, creamy without dairy, and with nothing added or taken away from the whole grain rice and culture it's made from.

It's a sweet rice food related to rice syrup, and has been used in Japan for centuries as the base of a delicious, warming drink. Amazake, literally 'sweet sake,' is made by fermenting cooked sweet rice with koji (rice with added Aspergillus culture) for six to ten hours. The surprisingly intense sweetness develops as the enzymes in the koji break down the complex starches in the rice into natural sugars. Amazake is high in fibre and complex carbohydrates, as well as the B vitamins niacin and thiamin, and is low in fat. It's a great food in terms of digestion, as the traditional fermentation process starts breaking down the complex whole grains into simpler, more easily digested nutrients. The first time you taste amazake, you won't believe that the sweet ambrosial flavour of this pudding comes entirely from cereal grain.

Clearspring's authentic, home-style Brown Rice Amazake is made by the Ryorido Company, in Zutphen, Holland. Ryorido's amazake is made from brown rice and rice koji using the same traditional fermentation methods that were used in the Japanese countryside before the industrial revolution. They also make Clearspring's unique and delicious Millet Amazake. Both the traditional brown rice and millet varieties are organic, dairy-free, gluten-free, and contain no sugar or processed ingredients.

Cooking with Amazake

For an alternative to porridge, try gently heating some amazake and serve with a little grated ginger. In winter, dilute it with hot water for a wholesome, warming drink. Cooled to room temperature or slightly chilled, this also makes a delicious summer drink. Experiment by blending seasonal fruits or a little carob powder into the amazake and water before heating, or add a few drops of vanilla extract before serving. Substituting rice, oat or almond drink for the water results in an extra delicious and creamy treat. Try the Almond Amazake Shake recipe here, and use this as a springboard for your imagination. The possibilities are limitless!

In addition to drinks such as shakes and smoothies, try using amazake in puddings and pie fillings, or in baked foods, including cakes, cookies, scones, muffins and bread. Amazake also adds sweetness to salad dressings... or simply eat some straight out of the jar.

Almond Amazake Shake

Serves 2

The key to the richness of this drink is the toasted almond butter. Ground almonds just don't do the trick.

240ml brown rice amazake

300ml almond milk or rice drink

a pinch of sea salt

3 tablespoons toasted almond butter

a few drops of natural vanilla extract

2 drops of natural almond extract

Purée all the ingredients thoroughly in a blender, pour into glasses, and put into the fridge. Serve this shake chilled.

For a super smooth texture, you can pour it through a fine-mesh strainer to remove any pieces of grain. If you do this, press the solids dry, and save them in a covered container in the fridge for adding to biscuit and cake recipes.

About the Contributors

John and Jan Belleme

John and Jan live in North Carolina, USA where they have written over a hundred articles about traditional Japanese foods. They studied how to make these foods in the countryside of Japan for a year, learning first-hand the intricate techniques behind everything from shoyu to seitan. John and Jan founded the American Miso Company, and have worked alongside Clearspring for many years.

Ysanne Spevack

Ysanne lives in central London, where she has written seven books about organic foods. Ysanne is editor of Organicfood.co.uk , the UK's top organic food magazine online, and is a regular contributor to many other magazines, including Food Illustrated and Organic Style. She lived in Japan for a short while, is a dab hand at eating with chopsticks, and loves umeboshi plums more than you can possibly imagine.

Montse Bradford

Montse is from Barcelona and lives in Somerset where she writes, advises on health and directs the Natural Cookery School. She is adept at incorporating Japanese ingredients into traditional European recipes. She has produced four titles in the Healthy Wholefood Cooking series and written four Spanish best-sellers on food and health. She can be contacted at *www.montsebradford.com*. Her recipes are marked with an asterisk.*

Useful Websites

Food

www.clearspring.co.uk   An overview of Clearspring's product range
www.goodnessdirect.co.uk   Mail order supplier of Clearspring foods
www.mitoku.com   More information on Clearspring's Japanese Foods
www.southrivermiso.com   The story of a craft miso maker
www.soyfoods.com   Soya foods information

Cooking and Lifestyle

www.montsebradford.com   Recipes and classes using Japanese foods

www.macrobioticcooking.com Cooking the macrobiotic way

www.macrobiotics.co.uk   A good introduction to macrobiotics

www.organicfood.co.uk   Organic magazine featuring Ysanne's writing

Japan

www.eat-japan.com   Exploring Japanese Food

www.jinjapan.org   Japan Information Network

www.teriyaki.co.uk   Directory of Japanese restaurants in the UK